THE
LITTLE
WAY
OF
LENT

meditations in the spirit of
St. Thérèse of Lisieux

FR. GARY CASTER

SERVANT
BOOKS

PUBLISHED BY ST. ANTHONY MESSENGER PRESS
CINCINNATI, OHIO

Excerpts from *Story of a Soul,* translated by John Clarke, O.C.D., copyright © 1975, 1976, 1996 by Washington Province of Discalced Carmelites, used by permission of ICS Publications, www.icspublications.org.

Unless otherwise noted, Scripture passages have been taken from the *Revised Standard Version,* Catholic edition. Copyright 1946, 1952, 1971 by the Division of Christian Education of the National Council of Churches of Christ in the USA. Used by permission. All rights reserved.

Note: The editors of this volume have made minor changes in capitalization to some of the Scripture quotations herein. Please consult the original source for proper capitalization.

Cover and book design by Mark Sullivan
Cover image copyright © Photodisc | Just Flowers

LIBRARY OF CONGRESS CATALOGING-IN-PUBLICATION DATA
Caster, Gary, 1961-
The little way of Lent : meditations in the spirit of St. Therese of Lisieux / Gary Caster.
p. cm.
Includes bibliographical references (p.   ) and index.
ISBN 978-0-86716-967-6 (pbk. : alk. paper) 1. Lent—Meditations. 2. Therese, de Lisieux, Saint, 1873-1897—Meditations. I. Title.
BX2170.L4C37 2010
242'.34—dc22

2010032824

ISBN 978-0-86716-967-6

Published by Servant Books, an imprint of St. Anthony Messenger Press.
28 W. Liberty St.
Cincinnati, OH 45202
www.AmericanCatholic.org
www.ServantBooks.org

Printed in the United States of America.

Printed on acid-free paper.

12 13 14 5 4

CONTENTS

INTRODUCTION

The autobiography of St. Thérèse of Lisieux, *The Story of a Soul*, tells of a young woman who "sailed on the waves of confidence and love."[1] Thérèse approached the spiritual life with absolute trust in God, and she described this as the little way of spiritual childhood. Her experience of the "incomprehensible condescension" of God's love[2] led her to embrace life positively, no matter the difficulties, frustrations, and trials. Free within God's love, she lived out her vocation as a Carmelite nun in gratitude and desired to do all things with great love.

St. Thérèse knew Jesus not as a stern and terrifying judge but as her "true love, her spouse, her only friend, her teacher and director."[3] He did not demand great things from her but guided her soul "with tenderness and sweetness."[4] She could therefore accept her weak and fragile status, "her littleness," with bold self-assurance.

Thérèse's confidence was rooted in the paschal mystery of Jesus' passion, resurrection, and ascension into heaven. She recognized in the "beautiful feast" of Christ's victory[5] that God's judgment on the world was perfectly exemplified through Jesus' self-offering. His sacrifice on the cross did not condemn the world but unleashed the mercy of God so that men and women could once again be united to him.

By uniting us with Jesus' forty days in the desert, Lent prepares us to celebrate the paschal mystery with gratitude and joy.

Through our communal fasts and days of abstinence, the Church encourages us to make Lent a special time of thoughtful reflection. The pious devotions associated with the season and the daily readings from sacred Scripture are meant to foster a deeper appreciation of Jesus' own self-offering.

The little way of spiritual childhood is a great help in fulfilling all that the Church proposes; it ensures that Lent will be a time from which we truly benefit. The disposition that characterizes it can lift the burden of concerns and preoccupations that typically make Lent forty days of drudgery. Absolute trust in God wards off feelings of spiritual inadequacy. And the vibrant confidence that St. Thérèse expresses can charge our minds and hearts to fully celebrate the resurrection of Christ.

Overcoming Fear

The first practical effect of the little way on the experience of Lent is a shift in focus. Instead of drawing our attention to human sinfulness, the fear of damnation, and the real horrors of hell, it keeps us firmly centered on the mercy of God.

It is nearly impossible to soar on eagle's wings (see Exodus 19:4) when weighed down by thoughts of personal failure and feelings of worthlessness. This far too common approach to Lent makes human behavior the center of attention and runs the risk of pushing Christ to the side. We must never forget that the paschal mystery does not expose that which man has done to offend God but that which God has done to redeem man. Lent is never about me, no matter how much I may have wronged the Lord; Lent is always about Christ Jesus and his sacrificial love.

Historically many gifted preachers have tried to draw their congregations' attention to what can be expected in the absence of true repentance. If and when Christ is mentioned, the focus is exclusively on his rejection, humiliation, and physical suffering. Many people think visceral descriptions of Jesus' physical torments can instill the necessary guilt that leads to genuine contrition.

In my experience both as a Christian and a priest, I have found two basic problems with approaching Lent from the perspective of fear. The first is a basic human truth: Fear cannot sustain a substantial, viable relationship. Conversions based on fear rarely last. Guilt and shame do not inspire love; they hinder it.

Human beings simply will not share or fully extend themselves to someone of whom they are afraid. Even if the thought of punishment instills obedience, it nonetheless causes a person to hold back from sincere relationship. This is a necessary means of self-protection. Jesus calls us "friends," not enemies (see John 15:14–15).

The second problem is that fear is not compatible with the language of the Church. While Lent is a solemn season, it is not a somber one. The forty days are not structured to foster morbid gloominess and debilitating self-loathing; they are meant to thrust us into the heart of divine love. This "communion," so beautifully and wonderfully expressed through the paschal mystery of Christ, is the cause of all joy and the reason for human hope.

All the saints have known this, and it is the reason why St. Paul preached "Christ, and him crucified" (1 Corinthians 1:23). He, like St. Thérèse, understood just what transpired on that fateful day on Calvary. This understanding made him a great apostle.

St. Thérèse searched Paul's words in order to discover her true place within the Church.

During my meditation, my desires caused me a veritable martyrdom, and I opened the Epistles of Saint Paul to find some kind of answer. Chapters 12 and 13 of the First Epistle to the Corinthians fell under my eyes. I read there, in the first of these chapters, that *all* cannot be apostles, prophets, doctors, etc., that the Church is composed of different members, and that the eye cannot be the hand at *one and the same time*.... Without becoming discouraged I continued my reading and this sentence consoled me: "Yet strive after THE BETTER GIFTS"...and the Apostle explains how *all the most PERFECT gifts* are nothing without LOVE. That Charity is the EXCELLENT WAY that leads most surely to God.... Charity gave me the key to my vocation.[6]

Rediscovering Sacrifice

The first preface of Lent describes these forty days as a "joyful season" that God has given us. The preface goes on to encourage reflection on "the great events that give us new life in Christ."[7] I am always surprised by the number of people shocked to learn this and saddened by the number who want to argue the point.

The reluctance to accept Lent as a season of joy seems to come from a misunderstanding of what it means to "offer something up." The thought of having to choose some form of penance and faithfully adhere to that choice casts the beginning of Lent in a negative light. Both young and old ask, "Why do I have to do this? Does God really care if I eat meat, chocolate, or candy, drink alcohol or soda, or smoke cigarettes?"

Many people dread giving something up because of personal failure. Without knowledge of the true purpose of sacrifice, failure shouldn't be a surprise. If we don't really know why we're doing something, we're sure to stop doing it!

The first thing we learn from the little way is that the act of offering something up has nothing to do with proving something to God. Finite, limited creatures could never prove anything to our infinite Creator. Rather we choose to offer something as a way of expressing our love for Christ and our gratitude for his suffering and death. It isn't the meat or the candy or the drink that matters; it's the human heart. The choice we make is not a rejection of something good; it is an opportunity to appreciate more intensely what Christ has done for us.

At the heart of the paschal mystery is God's desire to redeem us and make us his own. The best way to understand this is to consider our own desires. When we feel the tug or pull of whatever we have offered up, our feelings present an occasion to explore the nature of desiring. If something insignificant can really pull, then imagine the pull of a human life on God. Human beings are certainly more important than any of the things they offer up. Our physical yearning is like an icon that opens for us the mystery of the God who "thirsts for us."[8]

What I feel in my body enables me to contemplate what is wholly unimaginable and unheard of: God loves me! That is why the choice of our offering should be something significant, something that we will really miss.

Understanding the true purpose of our sacrifice prevents the pull or temptation to give in from overwhelming us. We no longer have to struggle through each day, hoping to mark it off the calendar as a sign of success. As our desires focus our attention on God's love, we begin to think of the sacrifices we're making in an entirely new way. In a sense we are also able to "feel" our love for God. This puts to rest anxious thoughts about how much longer we have before Lent ends so we can enjoy the things we have denied ourselves. Drawn into the mystery of God's love through our human desires, we may even wish Lent to never end! When it does, everything we have *felt* for forty days binds us to the passion of Christ in a way that no descriptive account of his suffering and death ever could.

In the season of Lent, the Church encourages us to "master our sinfulness and conquer our pride,"[9] but we are to do this within the context of thankfulness. The deeper our appreciation for what God has accomplished in Christ, the greater our gratitude. The sacrifices we make are simple ways of expressing thankfulness. God only asks us to accept his love in Christ Jesus.

The little way of spiritual childhood helps us begin Lent accepting our weak, fragile, and vulnerable condition. We are little before God, and that's all right. Failure is just a part of our human condition, so we can accept its possibility and move on in search of closer contact with the God who is steadfast in caring for us.

Since the little way fixes our attention on the person of Christ, it provides the right motivation for penance and self-denial. He is the one who "emptied himself, taking the form of a slave" (Philippians 2:7). The self-emptying of Christ, coupled with the self-emptying the Church encourages us to pursue during Lent, strengthens our bonds with God.

The Light of the Little Way

What I have found most appealing about St. Thérèse's approach to the spiritual life is its simplicity. She never sought to make herself something for God but chose to let God make of her something for him. This freed her to be herself and to embrace her family, others, and all of reality with lively interest and heartfelt appreciation. She had no worries about ascending to the heights of spiritual perfection. She expected Jesus himself to lift her up and place her there.[10]

During my first few years in the seminary, I imposed upon myself a rigorous asceticism, which always created a problem for me during Lent. It was difficult to offer something up because there wasn't much from which to choose. I wasn't eating meat, fish, or chicken. I didn't drink coffee, tea, or alcohol. I didn't smoke or eat baked goods or candy. About the only things I ate with any regularity were cucumber sandwiches. How could I offer something to God when I was already trying to give him all the things I enjoyed?

While rereading the autobiography of St. Thérèse, a new approach to the forty days came to me, one that has worked for me ever since. What struck me was her insistence on the *way* we do things for God and not the *things* we do for him. If I couldn't offer up the same thing for forty days, then I could choose something different each day and make that my offering. It wasn't about what I was offering; it was about *why* I was making an offering to God.

This awareness changed my life. I realized there was any number of things I could do each day to express my love in a tangible way. So now, during my time of prayer each morning of Lent, I share with the Lord the sacrifice I have in mind for that day. Some days God is kind enough to accept what I have chosen to offer him. On other days he has some other way for me to express my love.

This way of moving through the days of Lent has been a tremendous blessing. I can't remember the last time I felt the weight of having to go without something for forty days. And this approach keeps me continuously engaged. It has made the season of Lent exciting and, dare I say it, fun. It has changed the way I think about the Scripture readings and the lives of the biblical characters that are so much a part of our celebration of the paschal mystery.

When I entered the seminary, I promised St. Thérèse that, should I be ordained, I would try to bring people to her so that she might bring them to Christ. The meditations that follow, based on the lenten Mass readings, are all colored by her little way of spiritual childhood. At the beginning of each week is a pertinent quote from her writings, and at the end of each meditation is a shorter quote to aid your prayer and reflection.

St. Thérèse continues to look after me and spoil me with attention and affection, all the while encouraging me to be myself with God and to simply let him love me. It is my hope that you will let her do the same for you.

Beginning Lent

See then all that Jesus lays claim to from us; He has no need of our works but only of our *love*, for the same God who declares He has no need to tell us when He is hungry did not fear to beg for a little water from the Samaritan woman. He was thirsty. But when He said: *"Give me to drink,"* it was the *love* of His poor creature the Creator of the universe was seeking. He was thirsty for love.

Ash Wednesday
 First Reading: Joel 2:12–18
 Second Reading: 2 Corinthians 5:20—6:2
 Gospel: Matthew 6:1–6, 16–18

Understanding the Method

Lent is a favorable time for the Church community. Together the solemn assembly of God's people speak and act with one voice, crying out to God, "Spare your people, Lord!" This earnest invocation bursts forth from hearts broken open by the tenderness and compassion of God.

The sound that's heard is not the clamor of people calling attention to themselves or a summons to parade one's good deeds. It is more like the sound that will be heard when the angel announces the return of the Son of Man. The people rallying around the trumpet announcing Lent come together offering "oblations and libations" in gratitude, because the passion, death, resurrection, and ascension of the "one who knew not sin" has established once and for all time the day of salvation.

In the Gospel Jesus presents the method of these forty days. He encourages those assembled to bring his words to life through, with, and in terms of the unique conditions and circumstances of their lives. Prayer, fasting, and almsgiving are meant to impart renewed vitality to our personal acceptance of "God's appeal." Those who willingly yield to the method Jesus proposes know that reconciliation with God is never frightening. As Lent unfolds the effects of this reconciliation are felt in every facet of one's life.

The psalm response for today divulges the appropriate disposition for the method Jesus proposes. Being conscious of our weakness, frailty, and vulnerability allows us to reach out to God in prayer, to express our love for him through sacrifice, and to spend ourselves for others in love. Acknowledging our offenses moves us toward God and never away from him. The joy of our salvation depends upon our willingness to stand with confidence and cry out, "Be merciful, O Lord, for we have sinned!"

Jesus warns us that the good deeds done during Lent should be done *in secret*. There is little reason to tell anyone the sacrifices one has chosen to make, for certainly "your Father who sees in secret will reward you." "Winning the admiration of men" is not the goal or purpose of our sacrifices; expressing our love for God is.

The practices of these forty days should inspire our careful consideration of everything God has done for us and so draw us closer to him. More than just a time for "weeping and mourning" over our past, Lent is a time to accept with firm resolve the grace held out to us in Christ. It is a time for fixing our eyes on Jesus' paschal mystery and closing the door on all that distracts us and draws our attention away from the One in whom the Father has already rewarded us.

With you I shall sing the joy of serving Jesus and living in His house, the joy of being His spouse for time and Eternity.

Thursday After Ash Wednesday
First Reading: Deuteronomy 30:15–20
Gospel: Luke 9:22–25

What's Set Before Us?

Moses sets before the Israelites a choice between "life and prosperity, death and doom," with heaven and earth as witnesses. Keeping God's commandments guarantees life and security, so is there really any other choice? Before the Israelites can answer, Moses describes just what the choice for new, long, and abundant life will involve—"loving the LORD your God, / heeding his voice, and holding fast to him." Even this seems relatively easy.

Unfortunately, salvation history reveals how difficult loving the Lord, heeding his voice, and holding fast to him can be. The Israelites discovered this with great shame and true sorrow. While their original decision was heartfelt, the days would come when they wouldn't want to do what the Lord commanded. Sometimes the political, social, and religious character of other nations would be more appealing than that which Moses enjoined on them.

Many people who sincerely follow Christ experience times when personal preferences war against his teachings. Making accommodations with contemporary political, social, and religious sentiments can seem more beneficial than loving the Lord, heeding his voice, and holding fast to him. That's why Jesus presents self-denial as a condition of discipleship. It is impossible to follow God and oneself.

God has already charted the course for us and knows best how we can reach our destination. This way leads to a land promising more than milk and honey. Yet following the way of Christ demands exactly what was demanded of him: the cross.

People will argue that self-denial contradicts the notion of a loving God. Isn't saying no to myself unhealthy? Wouldn't a God of love want for me what I want for myself?

Not necessarily. We don't always know what's best for us. Jesus' own life reveals how God sees and loves in us more than we could ever see and love in ourselves. Jesus lays down his life precisely because sacrifice lies at the heart of any vibrant and fulfilling relationship. God's perspective is always greater than our own.

Self-denial makes sense within the context of love. In the presence of our beloved, self-denial becomes the means of genuine self-discovery. In looking on the one we love, we actually begin to see ourselves in new and healthier ways and are freed from the constraints of self-interest. This way of self-denial persistently enriches our lives, because it strengthens our ability to love the Lord, heed his voice, and hold fast to him.

How happy I am now for having deprived myself from the very beginning of my religious life.

Friday After Ash Wednesday
   First Reading: Isaiah 58:1–9a
   Gospel: Matthew 9:14–15

Recognizing Without Rejecting

Speaking on behalf of God, Isaiah is able to say things that only a prophet can say. Today his words are directed at the true nature of fasting, which makes them especially important as we begin the season of Lent.

The prophet describes, "full-throated and unsparingly," a picture of fasting that surpasses going without food, drink, or any other earthly good. Isaiah does so because all former approaches to fasting have ended in "quarreling and fighting, / striking with wicked claw." Is it any wonder God doesn't see his people's sacrifices? God is disturbed that his people only fast to get "what is due them." His hunger can only be satisfied by releasing the innocent, freeing the oppressed, feeding the hungry, sheltering the homeless, and clothing the naked.

The question asked by the disciples of St. John illustrates a lingering confusion about the true nature of fasting. Jesus affirms the words of Isaiah, stating in simple terms that fasting is ordered toward recognition and not rejection. The kind of fast God now asks of us depends entirely upon our recognition of the Bridegroom. Seeing Christ prevents us from feeding ourselves.

Fasting is all about recognition; it is all about the way we see Christ in others and therefore relate to them. Choosing to go without, choosing to deny ourselves some good, is supposed to open our minds and hearts to the true nature of desire. When we feel the pull of wanting something—whether it is food, shelter, freedom, love, or care—we can begin to understand God's longing to have us experience all the rich possibilities for which he created us. The more we understand how strongly God desires this, the easier and more welcome it is to keep "a day of penance."

Before the coming of the Bridegroom, the Israelites were deprived of the sustenance they needed. The plight of others should have been a reminder of their interior need for God. That's why Isaiah equated fasting with social responsibilities. The religious discipline was expected to reorient people's perspective, so that they could see that caring for others actually satisfied the internal hunger for God. Responding to the needs of others could heal the wounds caused by sin and secure God's abiding protection.

Now that Jesus has returned to the Father, fasting symbolizes our ever deepening hunger for God. It is more than a self-imposed religious practice; it is an expression of the longing for never ending communion with God. Fasting ensures that our sights stay fixed on eternal life and makes us appreciate more fully all the goods of the earth and the goodness in one another.

Love for mortification was given me, and this love was all the greater because I was allowed nothing by way of satisfying it.

Saturday After Ash Wednesday
  First Reading: Isaiah 58:9b–14
  Gospel: Luke 5:27–32

Spending for God
Giving alms has more to do with giving ourselves than with giving from our resources.

At a table where the scribes and Pharisees saw sin, Jesus saw possibility. He saw in Levi a man whose heart was ripe for managing the divine economy. Levi was made for something greater than earthly commerce. But in order to leave the tax collector's table, he had to divest himself of the illusory riches of the world.

Levi understood well the influence of earthly currency, but his heart ached for something richer and more profitable. He was captivated by a glance from Jesus that promised far greater returns than his business. Levi immediately set aside the now meaningless coinage of his day and committed himself instead to "giving alms" with Christ, to spending himself through love.

Once again the Gospel echoes the rich, vibrant language of Isaiah, who explained the economics proper to managing the household of God. We are called to "remove…oppression, / false accusation and malicious speech" and to "bestow…bread on the hungry / and satisfy the afflicted." Through our recognition of and response to the plight of others, the light of God will penetrate the darkness of the world.

Isaiah reminds us to "hold back" our feet on the Lord's Day, but keeping the Sabbath means more than that. On the seventh day God stepped back from his work so that we could step forward. The "rest" required by the Sabbath moves beyond the physical. It is a willed abstention that compels us to accept and accomplish our responsibility to all the living, rather than "following [our] own pursuits."

We have a sacred duty to manage the affairs of the world, because the earth has been given to us as our home. Although precious metals and gilded paper may be of assistance, they are never an accurate standard or correct measure. The divine household is managed by the giving and receiving of love, and this alone is the right standard for ordering the household of man. The measure with which we measure (see Mark 4:24; Luke 6:38) should always reflect the mutual, faithful, exclusive, and fruitful love of the Father, Son, and Holy Spirit.

While giving alms may sometimes require contributing what has been earned through human labor, the gift of oneself is of greater value. After all, the debt incurred by sin wasn't paid in the currency of the world but in the flesh of Christ. His self-sacrifice remains the greatest example of what it really means to give alms. Jesus will willingly "eat and drink with tax collectors and sinners" because he sees their bankrupt condition and has "the capital" necessary to restore them to full health.

I can see with joy that in loving Him the heart expands and can give to those who are dear to it incomparably more tenderness than if it had concentrated upon one egotistical and unfruitful love.

Week One

How great the power of *Prayer*.... To be heard it is not necessary to read from a book some beautiful formula composed for the occasion.... I do like children who do not know how to read, I say very simply to God what I wish to say, without composing beautiful sentences, and He always understands me. For me, prayer is an aspiration of the heart, it is a simple glance directed to heaven, it is a cry of gratitude and love in the midst of trial as well as joy; finally it is something great, supernatural, which expands my soul and unites me to Jesus.

Sunday, Week One, Cycle A
  First Reading: Genesis 2:7–9; 3:1–7
  Second Reading: Romans 5:12–19
  Gospel: Matthew 4:1–11

Living Up to Our Dignity

This first Sunday of Lent shows us that Satan's tactics never change. He lives to foster doubt and thereby distort reality. In the passage from the book of Genesis, he never tells Eve what to do; he simply encourages her to question God's word about "the tree in the middle of the garden." This confuses Eve. Has God really given her and Adam stewardship of creation? Using the goodness inherent in nature, Satan deceives the couple about the scope of human freedom.

He tries the same in the Gospel. Each temptation is nothing more than an attempt to use Jesus' humanity to confuse him. Questioning Jesus' power over nature raises doubts about the fullness of his divinity. Challenging God's providential care raises doubts about the goodness of Jesus' humanity. Offering Jesus all the kingdoms of the world raises doubts about whether the Father has already done so. Satan's method is blandly predictable; he cannot accept the fact that being human is not at odds with being one with God.

St. Thérèse could not be tricked by Satan, because she never doubted the goodness inherent in being human. Acknowledging her "littleness," her fragile and vulnerable humanity, was never a rejection of God's handiwork. This humility enabled her to hold steadfastly to what is written in sacred Scripture: "He will command his angels concerning you and with their hands they will support you." Knowing herself imperfect made her rely on the perfection of God. Her limitations led her to trust more deeply in his care.

Thus St. Thérèse saw the whole world as her own special garden. Rivers and streams, fish and birds, the clouds and stars in the sky, were all "desirable for knowledge of God." She walked in a world that sang God's praises. Nature opened her eyes to the dignity of her humanity, not its shame.

St. Thérèse saw and experienced reality through "the gracious gift of the one man Jesus Christ" that the Second Reading speaks of. She believed that Jesus had willingly exposed himself to the perils of mankind so that mankind could be exposed to the glories of God. She never put God to the test but tested herself. Where Satan thought he could have Jesus demand that the Father bend his will to the Son, Thérèse was content to continually bend her will to God's.

The season of Lent is about bending our will. It is about opening ourselves to the truth of reality, our own and that of creation. Lent is a time when, like St. Thérèse, we can shatter the deceptions of Satan by holding fast to the righteousness of Christ. Lent is a time for seeing that all of creation is good for guiding us to a greater knowledge of God.

The act of humility I had just performed put the devil to flight since he had perhaps thought that I would not dare admit my temptation. My doubts left me completely.

Sunday, Week One, Cycle B
  First Reading: Genesis 9:8–15
  Second Reading: 1 Peter 3:18–22
  Gospel: Mark 1:12–15

Standing in the Right Spot

Today St. Peter reminds us that the waters of the flood prefigure the waters of baptism. God always responds to human sinfulness by making things better. The waters of the flood were meant to recreate the world by cleansing it of sin. Unfortunately, it wasn't long before sin sprang back to life.

The same thing is true for those reborn through the waters of baptism. Although we become new creations, it isn't long before we fail to live up to the inherent dignity of our humanity. We may be washed clean and recreated by grace, but that doesn't guarantee the blameless conscience of which St. Peter speaks. How then do we find the way to interior peace?

The First Reading provides a fitting description. God sets a bow in the sky as a sign of his covenant with humanity and as a promise that he will never again destroy the earth, humanity's home. After the flood, when sin creeps back into the story of man's relationship with God, when failure seems a very apt explanation of human life, the bow in the sky could bring hope: God will not destroy! This truth guaranteed that there would always be a way back to God. He will never abandon us.

In today's Gospel we learn that in Christ—literally in his flesh and blood—God provides the perfect way back. When Jesus comes out of the desert after forty days of prayer and temptation, he boldly announces "the kingdom of God." He assures us that despite our failures, our imperfections, and even our sins, there is a way back to lived communion with God. We have only to repent, to turn toward him and take hold of his outstretched hand. In Jesus we will always find ourselves anew.

Repentance, the central theme of Lent, lies at the heart of the little way. St. Thérèse knew that the only way to be freed from the weakness, fragility, and vulnerability that often lead to sin is to turn to Jesus for everything. This confidence freed her to pray, speaking constantly with God; to fast, bending her will in little, hidden ways; and to give alms, spending herself on the needs of others. St. Thérèse didn't worry about making herself a saint; she left that difficult and complicated task to Jesus.

The hope once fostered by the sign of the rainbow has become in Christ a dynamic reality that reorders and transforms our lives. The waters of baptism place us in just the right spot for seeing ourselves, others, and all living things as God sees them. These waters literally place us within the life of Jesus, keeping us oriented toward God and neighbor.

St. Thérèse knew that the life we share with Christ is greater than the most spectacular rainbow. For she had discovered that sin, imperfection, and failure do not define us; Jesus does!

Sometimes I can't help smiling interiorly when I witness the change that takes place from one day to the next.

Sunday, Week One, Cycle C
First Reading: Deuteronomy 26:4–10
Second Reading: Romans 10:8–13
Gospel: Luke 4:1–13

The Way of Gratitude

Just as with Jesus, the devil is always awaiting another opportunity to put us to the test. In order to resist him, we have only to call "on the name of the Lord," as the reading from Romans assures us. It is really that simple.

Although it may seem as if Satan has greater power over us than he did over Jesus, the truth is otherwise. Jesus was truly tempted by the devil. Through his humanity he exposed himself to the same predictable yet powerful tricks Satan uses to destroy us, to put us to shame. During his time in the desert, he really hungered for God and the experience of being God's Son that had always been his. Yet it was by means of his humanity that Jesus could "confess with [his] mouth" the truth of God and thereby open for us the way of salvation.

What enabled Jesus to withstand the devil's tempting is revealed in the passage from Deuteronomy. Moses instructs the people of Israel on how they are to live their new life in the Promised Land. This life, ritually depicted in today's reading, must be firmly rooted in gratitude. The people must willingly and joyfully give back to the Lord the "firstfruits" of what he has given to them. They must always recall how everything they have is a direct result of the richness of God's mercy, for he saved them from "affliction,…toil, and…oppression" by the power of his "out-stretched arm."

What we learn from Jesus in the desert, we are called to put into practice during Lent. The ritual and personal practices undertaken during this solemn season should be fostered and fueled by our gratitude for that which God has given us in Christ. If we "believe in [our hearts] that God raised him from the dead," we will live in thankfulness and express it in every dimension of our lives. We will "not live on bread alone" or ever "put ... God to the test." We will adore God alone, for we know that his angels guard us in all our ways. Through the hunger of our lenten fasts, we will unite ourselves more firmly to Jesus, the Son who has delivered us and given glory to our humanity.

The entire life of St. Thérèse was an expression of gratitude. The Eucharist describes the single greatest characteristic of her life, thanksgiving. Each day she lived in a conscious sensitivity to what God had accomplished for her in the person of his Son. This was perfectly expressed in her desire to "win souls" for Jesus, to return to him the first fruits of her own desire and ability to love.

The little way is a way of saying through one's life, as does the responsorial psalm for this day, "My refuge and fortress, / my God, in whom I trust" (Psalm 91:2). The little way of St. Thérèse is the surest way to put the devil to flight, and it can be lived only by one who remembers all that the Lord in his goodness has done.

I felt how weak and imperfect I was and gratitude flooded my soul.

Monday of Week One
  First Reading: Leviticus 19:1–2, 11–18
  Gospel: Matthew 25:31–46

Prayer Fosters Communion

There is beautiful symmetry between today's reading from Leviticus and Jesus' description of the final judgment. This symmetry exposes the real nature of holiness by freeing it from the narrow ethical and moral characterizations that often lead to a preoccupation with one's own standing before God. As Moses tells the children of Israel, being holy as the Lord is holy is altogether determined by one's treatment of others. Their standing within the community of God's family will depend on to what extent they love their neighbor.

Jesus' words in the Gospel speak to something greater than mere social responsibilities. Those welcomed into the kingdom have fed, housed, clothed, visited, comforted, and cared for others. The Lord makes no mention of their moral purity or ethical perfection. These souls are perplexed. They weren't expecting to get something from God; they simply lived for others. This makes the question they ask Jesus, "When did we see you…?" one of the most beautiful in all of sacred Scripture, for it reveals absolute selflessness as the true hallmark of holiness.

Today's readings have important implications for the nature of prayer. Without a clear perception of human destiny, prayer too easily becomes a means to some personal end, and conversation with God one-sided. The accursed, shocked to learn that they have not ministered to the Lord, serve as an indictment against any reduction of prayer to simple obligation or the mere recitation of words. The accursed failed to understand that human destiny is communion with God *and* neighbor, not communion solely between the individual and God.

Genuine prayer comes from a deep longing for the type of communion Moses describes in Leviticus and Jesus addresses in today's Gospel. The longing for an impenetrable oneness with God *and* neighbor is naturally expressed both privately and with the rest of the assembly. Ongoing conversation with God opens us toward others without force, resentment, or the expectation of reward, while being attentive and responsive to others carries us right back to God. At the final judgment many will be shocked to learn that every facet of their lives had become prayer.

Human and divine communion is not only our destiny; it is the *explanation* of our existence. If personal prayer does not foster a greater sense of solidarity with others, it has most likely become the kind of posturing Jesus condemned on Ash Wednesday. Those who, through personal prayer and community worship, show that "the command[s] of the LORD" are consistent with all that is fundamentally human will never hesitate to feed and clothe, to shelter and visit, to comfort and console.

Oh! Infinite mercy of the Lord, who really wants to answer the prayers of His little children.

Tuesday of Week One
First Reading: Isaiah 55:10–11
Gospel: Matthew 6:7–15

Prayer Is Doing God's Will

In today's Gospel Jesus teaches the apostles *how* to pray. His words are more descriptive than proscriptive. He imposes them not as a rule but as a method.

The Church has long embraced the recitation of these words, for they are meant to fix within our minds the way toward intensive union with God. Only someone who longs to remain one with God and neighbor would ever be able to say and to mean, "Thy will be done." This sentence facilitates genuine and lasting prayer and is the foundation of Christian discipleship.

Accepting the will of God necessitates asking daily for the spiritual, emotional, and physical bread needed to faithfully carry it out. And since God's will is always aimed at building up his kingdom, we should be on the watch for anything that might tempt us to reconstruct it as our own. Daily we should ask for deliverance from all that distracts us, weighs us down, or confuses us about the things of God. These evils supplant God's will and seek to make his Word void. All our efforts to speak with and listen to God, whether alone or in the company of the Church, should have as a priority a greater willingness to say and to mean, "Thy Kingdom come."

The prophet Isaiah was already preparing the people for the communion with God that lies at the heart of Jesus' description of prayer. The people of Israel were encouraged to build their lives on the unshakable declaration that God's word does "not return…void." They observed the effectiveness of God's word in the signs and wonders he worked for them. Through their continuing relationship with God, they learned that whatever comes from his mouth will achieve the end for which he sent it.

God's Word has been given to us as both the grammar and the vocabulary for sustained conversation. When his Word took flesh in Christ, the conversation between God and the human family became wonderfully personal: It is now mutual and reciprocal. Our incorporation into the body of Christ permits us to really speak with and listen to God and not "babble like the pagans."

In Christ God speaks *to* each one of us, not *at* us. Jesus is the definitive sign and greatest wonder that has ever come forth from God, because he brings us into perpetual conversation with God. Through Christ we gain a hearing with God, not because of the number of our words or the frequency with which we speak them but because of the honesty and the intensity with which we can say, "Thy will be done."

Sometimes when my mind is in such great aridity that it is impossible to draw forth one single thought to unite me with God, I very slowly recite an "Our Father."

Wednesday of Week One
  First Reading: Jonah 3:1–10
  Gospel: Luke 11:29–32

Prayer Is Life

Every generation seeks a sign, a confirmation: God should demonstrate whether or not he agrees with a decision, action, or goal. This can make the content of prayer largely self-serving and even an attempt at controlling God. We think he is supposed to protect us from harm, preserve us from pain and suffering, and shelter us from tragedy. We expect him to be ever ready to act in a way that proves that he cares and is involved. This is what the audience in today's Gospel wants.

Sadly, there is no external sign that can satisfy our desire for certainty. Putting God to the test always ends with human disappointment. The king of Nineveh, in the reading from Jonah, knew better. When news of the forthcoming destruction and the people's fast reached him, "he laid aside his robe, covered himself in sackcloth, and sat in the ashes." He didn't question Jonah or second-guess the Lord. He knew the only hope of salvation for him and his people was to return to God.

One measure of a healthy life of prayer is that it never seeks a sign. Prayer should never be an effort to control or manipulate how God acts in our lives; it is not a means to an end but an end in itself. The wisdom Jesus references in the Gospel pertains to this. When we know that doing the Lord's bidding is the only way to be fully alive, we can be sure that we have recognized the "greater than Solomon" who is in our midst.

Thus there is a sense in which, as Jesus says, it is "evil" to ask for a sign from God. How can we ask him to prove or confirm a decision, an action, or a goal when he has already confirmed his love and care for us in the passion, death, resurrection, and ascension of his Son? The ongoing interior conversation generated by the paschal mystery is intended to preserve us from the insecurity that gives rise to making demands of God. The life of Jesus is far greater than the preaching of Jonah. Do we truly recognize this?

The forty days of Lent are not meant to end in destruction. The signs given to us throughout these solemn days all point toward God's redemptive love. As Jesus went about the three years of his public ministry, doing the bidding of God, he was announcing something unimagined and unexpected. In him God "repented of the evil that he had threatened." God wants no one to perish but wants everyone to return to him and live.

I offered myself to Jesus in order to accomplish His will perfectly in me without creatures ever being able to place any obstacle in the way.

Thursday of Week One
First Reading: Esther C:12, 14–16, 23–25
Gospel: Matthew 7:7–12

God Is Not an ATM

The "mortal anguish" of Queen Esther is a fitting description of the heart that fears being separated from God. There is only one way that mourning can be turned into gladness, and that is by having constant recourse to the Lord. Like Esther, we should entrust the whole of our lives to God's providential care. Her prayer brings passion to the words of today's responsorial psalm, for it is a great example of what it means to pray "with all [one's] heart" (Psalm 138). The Lord hears the words of Esther's mouth and gives her what she asks for, because she knows that he is always true to his name and his promises.

The prayer of Esther sheds light on the type of asking, seeking, and knocking that Jesus has in mind in today's Gospel. He is not encouraging the disciples to make requests of the Father based on their assessment of what's needed. Nor is he encouraging their prayer to be a continuing series of petitions that anticipate God's attention. These two approaches to prayer, while common, are ultimately shallow. Prayer should never focus exclusively on personal needs. God is not a spiritual ATM! As we have already been reminded, he knows what we need even before we ask him (see Matthew 6:8).

Prayer should be an active expression of wanting to remain intimately united with God, the always urgent plea that *his* will be done. The only request that should ever be made of God is that he provide whatever is needed to carry out his will. We should *ask* for the tools and the strength needed. We should *seek* out the people and spiritual practices that will cultivate our union with God. We should *knock* on those doors that open into the household of the living God and expect to be given "bread and fish" and every other good thing that will sustain us.

Thankfully, the Church provides us with the right community of people and with efficacious spiritual practices. She opens the doorway for the King of Glory, so that he may enter into our lives and dwell within us. The Church reminds us that we are not orphans but members of God's family. Through her maternal care and wise instruction, she "[builds] up strength" within us. She relentlessly reminds us that we are the handiwork of God and that he will never forsake us.

When we realize our complete and total dependence on God, then he will answer us, as he did Queen Esther, whenever we call. Our prayers should originate in our neediness, our "littleness." We should give thanks and sing God's praises because we know that he will complete the work he has begun in us. We can cry out to God "from morning until evening" because we live within his loving kindness and know that he would never hand us a stone in place of a loaf or a snake in place of a fish.

He teaches us that it is enough to knock and it will be opened, to seek in order to find, and to hold out one's hand humbly to receive what is asked for.

Friday of Week One
First Reading: Ezekiel 18:21–28
Gospel: Matthew 5:20–26

Prayer at the Altar

Too often it can seem as if the greatest obstacle to loving one's neighbors is the neighbors. Intemperate, unfaithful, vulgar, immoral, and just plain selfish people are difficult to love. Perhaps if they were better Christians, "keeping God's statutes and doing what is right and just," it would be effortless to love them.

Yet a lack of love prohibits genuine prayer and stains whatever is offered to God. That's why Jesus tethers loving one's neighbor to the altar. No gift should be brought before God if the heart of the giver is weighed down by problems with his brother. Concerns about "an opponent" prevent our gifts from being the best we have to give. We can't make a suitable offering to God until all conflicts and anxious worries have been settled.

Note that Jesus also tethers anger to the commandment against killing. The frustrations that give rise to anger usually stem from not being treated as one would like. The failure of another to satisfy our expectations can instill deep-seated resentments, which really just fuel the fires of Gehenna. Cain should have realized this before he killed his brother. Abel wasn't the problem at all; Cain's offering was.

A selfless offering is a fruit born of prayer that has become communion with God. If my sole desire is to serve the Lord, then I will never become unduly attached to anyone or anything. Selflessness allows for right relationships between oneself and God and between oneself and one's neighbor. It is a sign that one has turned "from all the sins that he committed" in order to do "what is right and just," as Ezekiel advises. Selflessness awakens me to the truth that the flaws of others are no more an obstacle to loving them than are my own. Being able to see others from the divine perspective lets me respond to them in a way that is similar to God's merciful response to me.

Today's responsorial psalm presents the only true and certain way to turn from iniquity: we are to fix our minds and hearts on God and "[trust] in his word" (Psalm 130:5). Centering our lives on the gravitational pull of Christ makes us open and responsive to others. There is no hesitation in trying to do whatever we can for someone, even if all we can do is pray.

Living out the two great commandments doesn't oblige me to become friends with the entire body of Christ; it obliges me to stop marking their iniquities and to instead help them stand before the Lord. As long as our life of prayer remains focused on furthering union with God, it will become a source of hope for others, and our gifts at the altar will be accepted.

When Jesus gave His Apostles a new commandment,... it is no longer a question of loving one's neighbor as oneself but of loving them as He, Jesus has loved him.

Saturday of Week One
    First Reading: Deuteronomy 26:16–19
    Gospel: Matthew 5:43–48

Being Perfectly Human

The First Reading reminds us that those who follow the law of the Lord are truly blessed. If we "walk in his ways and observe his statutes, commandments and decrees, and hearken to his voice," then God will secure for us "praise and renown and glory." Observing the precepts of the Lord with all our heart and all our soul makes us "sacred to the LORD."

Through the statutes and decrees handed down by Moses, God prepared the hearts of his people to once again experience the essence of what it is to be human. In the Gospel Jesus describes this as being "children of your heavenly Father." Although the Law had no power of adoption, it was able to form the hearts and minds of those who followed it for the grace that would be given in Christ.

Thus Jesus both affirms and expands the Law. The essence of being human is conveyed through a love that takes us beyond what the Law instructed. Where previously the Law prepared the human heart for God's redemptive love, in Christ the human heart is wholly transformed. The commands of the Lord are no longer imposed from without; they operate naturally within the lives of God's adopted children. This transformation, which is the primary work of grace, makes loving enemies and praying for persecutors really possible—not as an obligation but as an honest expression of the heart.

At the conclusion of today's Gospel, Jesus sums this up in the most unusual way. He tells his disciples to be perfect, "just as your heavenly Father is perfect." But how is it possible for limited, fragile creatures to live without imperfection or sin?

In the words of the responsorial psalm we find the answer. We must "walk in the law of the LORD" (Psalm 119:1). What Jesus demands of his disciples is not impossible, because he is simply asking them to walk with him. His words are aimed not at ethical norms but at our willingness to adhere to his life in us. He expects his disciples to act in accord with the truth of how they were made, in the image and likeness of God. God always acts according to his nature. He is perfect, and he is love. Jesus is really telling his disciples, "Always be human!"

Of course, the secret to being human is only found in God; it is never the outcome of our own initiatives, actions, or ideas. In today's Gospel Jesus assures us that we can live the dignity that is naturally ours and supernaturally given by walking in his ways, observing his decrees, and seeking him with all our hearts.

It is only charity that can expand my heart. O Jesus, since this sweet flame consumes it, I run with joy in the way of Your NEW commandment.

WEEK TWO

My one purpose, then, would be to accomplish the will of God, to sacrifice myself for Him in the way that would please Him.

Sunday, Week Two, Cycle A
First Reading: Genesis 12:1–4a
Second Reading: 2 Timothy 1:8b–10
Gospel: Matthew 17:1–9

The Vision From the Mountain

God calls each one of us, just as he did Abram, to leave "the land of [our] kinsfolk" and go to a land that he will show us. Our native dwelling place, disordered by the original sin of our first parents, cannot sustain human life. The season of Lent reminds us that our present life is but a journey, an ongoing movement toward a place where death is robbed of its power, a place where our faces will be as dazzling as the sun and our clothes as radiant as light.

Paul tells Timothy, in the Second Reading, that already grace is "bestowed on us in Christ." Through, with, and in him we are moving toward "a holy life," not because of any merit of ours but because this has been part of God's design since "before time began."

This great destiny has been secured for us by the "hardship" Christ endured. The light of the Transfiguration isn't exclusively for Peter, James, and John but for all men and women, that we might no longer be afraid of our fragile, fallen humanity but might get up and go where the Lord is leading us. The words from the cloud, "This is my beloved," are spoken for "all the communities of the earth." People everywhere will find blessing in the Savior.

The conversation between Jesus, Moses, and Elijah forms a stunning depiction of prayer as communion. Speaking with Christ is a multifaceted engagement with those who have done as the Lord directed. Its singular purpose is to bring into ever-clearer light the life and immortality of the Gospel. This type of prayer expands our understanding of God's design and strengthens us to "bear [our] share of hardship," so that everyone might rest the mercy of the Lord of which the psalm response speaks.

St. Thérèse understood how the Transfiguration of Jesus shines light upon the true essence of our humanity. She allowed the truth of that moment to encompass her life and lived with a hope secured by complete trust in the paschal mystery. Her life became the type of lived communion the disciples witnessed on the mountain. This communion prompted her to make love incarnate in the most ordinary moments of her life. She heard the "voice from the clouds" and surrendered her life to the truth to which it testified.

Throughout these forty days the Church makes known the vision from the mountain in different ways, so that we too can hear it. God has indeed called us to a holy life. We can continue our journey toward the place he has prepared, because we know—with Peter, James, John, and St. Paul—that God's favor rests on us all.

Yes, all is well when one seeks only the will of Jesus.

Sunday, Week Two, Cycle B
   First Reading: Genesis 22:1–2, 9a, 10–13, 15–18
   Second Reading: Romans 8:31b–34
   Gospel: Mark 9:2–10

How Good It Is to Be Here

On a height that God selected, Abraham learned what every Christian should never take for granted: God is for us! When Abraham lifted his knife, he did so in absolute obedience and with complete trust. He believed even though he was one of those "greatly afflicted" whom the Responsorial Psalm refers to (Psalm 116:10), because God had always been true to his word.

It was good that Abraham was on that mountain, for there was revealed the height and depth and breadth of his love of God. This experience became the foundation for everything God hoped to accomplish through Abraham and for everything God would accomplish through the Son he would not spare. Abraham's willingness to slaughter his beloved son became the defining moment of his relationship with God, for through it he learned that his love for God was real.

Peter, James, and John would learn that God's love for us is real when God's own Son was handed over. On the mountain to which Jesus took them, they were being prepared to recognize that the Lamb of sacrifice and the man whom they were following were one and the same. On that mountain they learned what it means to walk in the presence of the Lord.

It was good for them to be there, so that they could witness that God does not "bring a charge" against us, as Paul says in the Second Reading, nor does his Son condemn us. After the Resurrection they would tell everyone of this moment on the mountain, just as their ancestors passed down Abraham's story from the mountain.

Spiritually speaking, the scriptural readings and practices of Lent are meant to take us up to a height that God has chosen. There we stand with Abraham, Peter, James, and John, so that we can learn for ourselves the degree to which we truly love God. The things we offer and the prayers we say open us to the truth of the words spoken from the cloud.

The mountain we ascend during Lent is actually a hill outside Jerusalem called the Place of the Skull. When we willingly offer to God all that is most beloved, we stand at the altar of the cross and learn just how "precious" we are "in the eyes of the LORD" (Psalm 116:15).

St. Thérèse learned and lived Abraham's lesson from the mountain. Her weak, fallen flesh was transfigured by the conviction of two great loves: God's love for her and her love for God. Her absolute obedience and complete trust were expressed with St. Paul's conviction that God "will give us everything else along with him." Her life was a perpetual sacrifice of thanksgiving, for in her own unique existence, she knew what "rising from the dead" meant.

I felt as did St. Paul, that nothing could separate us from the Divine Being who so ravished me!

Sunday, Week Two, Cycle C
First Reading: Genesis 15:5–12, 17–18
Second Reading: Philippians 3:17—4:1
Gospel: Luke 9:28b–36

God Manages the Outcome
Both the First Reading and the Gospel indicate that prayer, intimate personal conversation with God, is ultimately a mystery. God manages the experiences we have when we open ourselves to him. Any attempt to manufacture what occurs or determine the outcome is not only futile but selfish. The gifts we bring and the sacrifices we make, our equivalent of the three-year-old heifers, she-goats, and rams, cannot force the hand of God. Like Abraham, we have to put our faith in the Lord, for this alone is "an act of righteousness."

The trance that came upon Abraham and the deep sleep into which the apostles fell are both examples of prayer. They demonstrate the truth of St. Paul's words to the Philippians that "our citizenship is in heaven." Through the communion with God established by our Savior, the barrier between the material and spiritual orders has been torn down, literally (see Matthew 27:51). The things of this world should not control or limit our thoughts; rather, thoughts of higher things should determine the things of this world. Although we await a new form for our lowly bodies, we can even now stand firm with Moses, Elijah, Peter, James, John, St. Paul, and all the holy ones.

On the mountain we also learn with the disciples that the covenant between God and Abraham was but the first movement in God's plan to redeem humanity. That initial bond would be expressed in a richer, more personal way by Jesus' self-offering on the cross. In his conversation with Moses and Elijah, Jesus discusses his impending sacrifice, a sacrifice that will ensure that no other human will ever have to pay for sin. This gift of his life to the Father makes of our lives something they could never be before: real and fitting offerings. By his death every facet of our lives can become an appropriate expression of our love of God.

This is the essential insight of St. Thérèse's spirituality. Everything she did and all that she experienced expressed her love of God. She knew that even the most mundane chore and smallest act of self-denial was "consumed" by the paschal mystery and presented to God. She knew that her personal history had become interwoven with the way God has chosen to redeem humanity. The value of her prayer was that it was the primary method through which God continually expressed his love for her and manifested his presence.

After the mysterious experience on the mountain, Jesus was there alone. This affirms that he is the one mediator by which we have access to heaven, to the life of God. The prayer championed by the little way of St. Thérèse directs our vision to the stars of the sky that God showed Abraham. It leads us to live beneath the cloud from which the Father's voice rings out, accepting all that we offer.

He has always given me what I desire or rather He has made me desire what He wants to give me.

Monday, Week Two
First Reading: Daniel 9:4b–10
Gospel: Luke 6:36–38

Prayer Without Measure

The powerful words of the prophet Daniel continue to develop and reinforce the nature of true prayer. He simply and truthfully talks to God about the "shamefaced" condition of his people. What he describes is painful. The people, and here Daniel includes himself, have "sinned, been wicked and done evil." They have rebelled and departed from God's commandments and his laws. Daniel knows that justice is surely on the Lord's side!

Yet there is a sense of poise and self-assurance in what he says. Daniel can be frank with God, because he knows that the Lord is "great and awesome," that he keeps his "merciful covenant" toward those who obey him. Daniel knows that God will act and that whatever decision he makes will truly benefit his people. Daniel loves and respects God, and this makes his confession a prayer of thanksgiving.

Every confession should be like Daniel's. The confession of our sins should come as an honest and heartfelt response to God's greatness and compassion. We should be willing to accept whatever his justice decides, knowing that the punishment we receive is itself a sign of his redemptive mercy.

Daniel teaches us to pray with confidence and confess with hope. He knew the people didn't deserve God's mercy, but he also knew that God doesn't measure things the way we do. God never deals with us as our sins deserve. The paschal mystery we are preparing to celebrate confirms this truth.

God measures according to the love that constitutes his life. His desire that we share his life surpasses even our sinfulness. God does not judge, nor does he condemn; God forgives! The proof of this is in the full measure of good gifts that he has poured into our laps through Jesus his Son.

Today Daniel helps us to see prayer from God's perspective. True prayer requires radical acceptance of God's love, which in turn undoes every selfish preoccupation. The loftiness of prayer is not determined by our great efforts but by our willingness to capitulate to God's love. His love forms and colors the words we speak to him.

The words of Jesus in today's Gospel are the perfect ending to Daniel's prayer. What is mercy but the refusal to deal with others as their sins deserve? Jesus can insist that his followers stop judging and condemning, because the human standard must be the measure with which God measures.

The paschal mystery reveals God's judgment on the world in the overwhelming torrent of love that flows from the wounded heart of Christ. This life-giving water has freed those doomed to death and has made the cross the definitive standard of both divine and human love.

To lend without hoping for anything appears difficult to nature.... How contrary are the teachings of Jesus to the feelings of nature!

Tuesday of Week Two
First Reading: Isaiah 1:10, 16–20
Gospel: Matthew 23:1–12

Listening and Learning

At the beginning of Lent, Jesus taught us the method for these forty days. Our spiritual practices should be determined by the Son of God, whose life of prayer expressed communion with the Father. Through the gift of the Spirit, our prayer is also meant to express communion. We are not to "babble" or to multiply words (see Matthew 6:7). We are to go to our rooms, close the door, and withdraw into our inner hearts.

This type of prayer assures the promises made by the prophet Isaiah. Our sins can "become white as wool." We can "eat the good things of the land" if we "set things right"! In the interior of the heart our "one Father in heaven" establishes a conversation with us that heals, strengthens, and purifies. Through this conversation Jesus, our "one teacher," instructs our minds and lifts our burdens. Through our conversation with him, we learn how to serve others, because our one "Master" does not call us slaves but friends.

As Jesus guides and instructs us, every work and struggle, every joy and pain, becomes a means of praising him, such that knowledge of the Lord and his ways comes to us as pure gift. Gently, without force or struggle, we penetrate the deepest mysteries of faith. The Spirit working within fosters new insights and heightens our appetite to "redress the wronged, / hear the orphan's plea, defend the widow."

One sign of this is an awakened appreciation of sacred Scripture. The choice to read Scripture regularly and more thoughtfully is born from a need to have a richer and wider vocabulary in our conversation with God. The sacred words merge with our own, so that we are better able to speak with and about the Word himself.

This in turn moves us to study the teachings of the faith—not to master the sacred mysteries but to serve them. Reading and reflecting upon these truths, we become ever more caught up in the work of God's Word within. Through study and reflection we see our lives in the context of these savings truths and experience all of reality with wonder and in joy.

The more prayer becomes expressive of intimate communion with God, the greater our hunger to know the One whose life we share sacramentally. The sacred character of the Mass no longer depends upon the celebrant, the music, or the setting. Rather we find that every gesture, posture, and prayer is a gift. The order of the Mass spills into the events of our lives, uniting the liturgy of the divine with the liturgy of the ordinary.

Ah! Had the learned who spent their life in study come to me, undoubtedly they would have been astonished to see a child of fourteen understand perfection's secrets.

Wednesday, Week Two
First Reading: Jeremiah 18:18–20
Gospel: Matthew 20:17–28

Prayer and Suffering

In the First Reading, rather than listen to the prophet's radical vision of God, the people contrive a plot against Jeremiah. In the Gospel Jesus warns the twelve as they head toward Jerusalem that "the chief priest and the scribes…will condemn him to death, and hand him over to the Gentiles to be mocked and scourged and crucified." The fate of both men seems to prove the lament that good is often repaid by evil.

Aware of this, the mother of the sons of Zebedee wants some assurance that her children's sacrifices will be richly rewarded. What mother wouldn't? Jesus knows she's being not impertinent but protective, and he uses her request to reveal something completely unthinkable—namely, that "the Son of Man did not come to be served but to serve and to give his life as a ransom for many."

Jesus is not afraid of dying in order to fulfill God's plan. Everyone who follows him will "drink the chalice." Accepting this cup is a sign of one's willingness to serve and to suffer. The demands of discipleship can seem frightening and cause our prayer to remain shallow. Why must we drink from his chalice?

The conversation recorded in the Gospel holds the answer. Jesus didn't come to alleviate human suffering but to transform it. Sin frustrates the work that properly belongs to man, and man pays the price through natural disasters, illness, pain, violence, injustice, and finally death. But the body assumed by the Son of Man changes all of this.

Our physical, biological life here and now has the chance to experience salvation within. This is a great gift, far better even than sitting at the right or the left in Jesus' kingdom. Although we can suffer and we will die, Christ allows us an actual and substantial awareness of redemptive love, robbing suffering and death of their debilitating character. Instead of asking to be delivered from suffering and death, we can be grateful for them as avenues to deeper union with God.

Many saints thus testified to a willingness to suffer. They were not psychologically ill or morbidly curious; they wanted their union with Christ to be complete. Their deep personal prayer allowed them to see the far-reaching implications of the crucifixion of the Son of Man. Jesus' death on the cross was the perfect means of bringing the human family into the family of God.

Once we come to know suffering from God's perspective, the words of Psalm 116 can truly become our own:

> How shall I make a return to the LORD
> for all the good he has done for me?
> The cup of salvation I will take up,
> and I will call upon the name of the LORD.

I desire to suffer for love and even to rejoice through love.

Thursday, Week Two
  First Reading: Jeremiah 17:5–10
  Gospel: Luke 16:19–31

Which Side Are We On?
The striking parable about the rich man and Lazarus the beggar, addressed to the Pharisees, has more to do with the here and now than with the hereafter. Jesus has come into the world so that we can partake in the intimate, loving communion that defines the life of God. As the Scriptures remind us, we are called to love our neighbors, not just see them. The rich man never learned this. Even in death he fails to grasp the responsibility he had toward Lazarus, his neighbor.

By describing the chasm that exists between the "bosom" of Abraham and the "netherworld," where the rich man resides, Jesus asserts that our future is determined by our present. When our time on earth is up, we will be forever the way we have chosen to be. If we haven't learned this already, chances are we never will—even should a man come back from the dead.

Through this parable Jesus widens the scope of his connection to the Old Testament prophets. As we heard in yesterday's Gospel, the Son of Man will rise on the third day in order to fulfill the Law and the prophets, not change them. The Resurrection confirms the truth of everything Jesus says about God and the essence of being human. His presence has far-reaching implications for the here and now, and genuine prayer has everything to do with noticing the implications.

The first thing to notice is that union with God demands utter trust in Christ. As Jeremiah says in the First Reading, "Cursed is the man who trusts in human beings, / who seeks his strength in flesh."

We notice too that our insistence on autonomy creates hell for ourselves and others and that sin increases our separation from God. In our sin we are "like a barren bush in the desert," standing "in a lava waste, / a salt and empty earth." Our flesh cannot fulfill us, regardless of our "fine linen" and "sumptuous" meals.

In the resurrection of Jesus from the dead, we see that God is not content with the "chasm" formed by the original demand for human autonomy, which brought sin and death into the world. God offers his own life in an act of mercy that shatters the hardness of the human heart. The inexhaustible love of God refuses to be silenced, stamped out, or pushed aside. In the resurrection of Jesus, God has responded to our impoverished condition—not with fragments, crumbs, or leftovers but with the abundant riches of his life.

This is the way God sees fit to take care of me.

Friday, Week Two

First Reading: Genesis 37:3–4, 12–13a, 17–28a

Gospel: Matthew 21:33–43, 45–46

Revealed From Above

Prayer should always be an occasion to "remember the marvels the Lord has done" for us, as the Responsorial Psalm instructs us (Psalm 105:5a). The time we set aside each day to speak with and listen to God should include the kind of remembering that takes place during Mass. After the words of institution, the anamnesis literally joins us to the passion, resurrection, and ascension of Christ. The words recited by the priest don't merely recall something that happened in the past; through the power of the Holy Spirit, they bring the past and present together.

The way we remember at Mass discloses the capacity in us called conscience, which enables us to be connected with our Creator. This aptitude is uniquely human and is the basis for morality. Our identity is rooted in the God who created us, and forgetting who we are always leads to sin.

In the First Reading the brothers of Joseph not only show us what happens when we forget God; they also show us what happens when we let our feelings determine reality. Only two of them exercise their consciences: Reuben encourages them to throw Joseph into a cistern, from which he hopes to rescue him later; Judah reminds his brothers that Joseph is "our own flesh" and suggests selling him to the Ishmaelites rather than killing him. Jealousy and hatred have quieted the consciences of Israel's other sons.

The tenants in today's Gospel also have a memory problem. They are so enamored of the fruits of their labor that they forget their responsibility to the landowner. They beat, kill, and stone his servants, and they kill his son. They have forgotten who they are, and they allow their passions to define reality.

The chief priests and the Pharisees know that Jesus is speaking about them, but they continue to let emotion—in this case fear—determine their behavior. Each one's conscience is "weighed … down with fetters" and "bound with chains" of ignorance. Jesus tries to release them, but they persist in their defiance. They have already made up their minds concerning Jesus. They have forgotten God, so the kingdom of God will rightly be taken away from them.

Our times of prayer should be times of "remembering" God. It is important not to focus on our emotions or anxious concerns. God wants us to bring ourselves to him as we are so that we can see our lives from his distinctive perspective. Through our interior conversation we "remember" the goodness, truth, and beauty of our humanity, without the conditions and circumstances that so often cause us to forget them. Conscience connects us with the Father. In him we can see how everything we do must correspond with the nature he has given us.

After considering the power of Almighty God, I had the opportunity of admiring the power he has bestowed in His creatures.

Saturday of Week Two
  First Reading: Micah 7:14–15, 18–20
  Gospel: Luke 15:1–3, 11–32

The Way Home

Being exceedingly familiar with Jesus' parables sometimes poses a problem. We can forget essential words, phrases, and details. The parable of the Prodigal Son is a good example of this. Most people forget that Jesus is speaking to the Pharisees and scribes, who have provoked Jesus by their harsh exclusivity: "This man welcomes sinners and eats with them."

The judgment they make about the company Jesus keeps shows their ignorance of God. They keep themselves clean because they consider it a way to gain favor with God. They have forgotten that God "removes guilt / and pardons sin," as the prophet Micah tells us in the First Reading. Rather the Pharisees and scribes seek to do this on their own. God is not the master of their spiritual lives. They might be members of God's family, but they have forgotten just who their Father is.

Jesus tries to remind them that the God of Abraham and Jacob is "kind and merciful," as Psalm 103 tells us today, casting into the depths of the sea all our sins. The actions of the father in the parable flesh this out. He doesn't argue, fight, or plead with his son to stay. He gives him what is asked for and lets him find his way. The father is so confident he has planted the truth firmly in the heart of his son that he goes out each day expecting him to return!

Amid the squalor of a pigsty, the son remembers the truth of his origins. His memory presents a picture of goodness that extends even to the servants. No longer forgetful of the benefits of home, he sees that his sins, failings, and transgressions do not define him. His father's love is greater than his wrongdoing. This fact compels him to get up and go back. And when he returns, his father does not chide him; he clothes him in a fine robe and orders a feast.

The older brother forgets himself, literally. He is angered by the reception and takes no delight in the father's clemency. He refuses to enter the house and to rejoice in his brother's salvation.

The father comes looking for his oldest son, just as he had the younger one. He invites his boy in, only to hear of how this son has lived in obedient servitude and not in love. Like the scribes and the Pharisees, the older son can't fathom what's taking place because he has forgotten just who his father is.

The younger son was right to return. His sins do not define him; he is always his father's son. This is the truth revealed by Jesus' choice of dinner companions. He welcomes them because he wants to reawaken the truth within their hearts that they are God's children.

Like the father in the story, God does not want us to spend our lives in filth and squalor. He wants to clothe and feed us and have us always with him. Prayer keeps us home and prevents us from forgetting who we really are.

You have said to me as the father of the prodigal son said to his older son: "EVERYTHING that is mine is yours."

WEEK THREE

I made a resolution to give myself up more than ever to a *serious* and *mortified* life. When I say mortified, this is not to give the impression that I performed acts of penance. *Alas, I never made any....* My mortifications consisted in breaking my will, always so ready to impose itself on others, in holding back a reply, in rendering little services without any recognition, in not leaning my back against a support when seated, etc., etc. It was through the practice of these *nothings* that I prepared myself to become the fiancée of Jesus.

Sunday, Week Three, Cycle A
  First Reading: Exodus 17:3–7
  Second Reading: Romans 5:1–2, 5–8
  Gospel: John 4:5–42

Going to the Well

We shouldn't be too quick to criticize the Israelites for their complaints. The expectation that God would always provide them with exactly what they needed was fostered by the remarkable signs and wonders he worked in freeing them from slavery in Egypt. Their demand for water is really a demand to know that God still cares about their well-being. God demonstrates again that he will not abandon them as they journey toward the Promised Land.

At some point we've all experienced physical hunger and intense thirst. Rarely are these human desires connected with spiritual ones. Yet Jesus makes that connection in today's Gospel. The woman he meets at the well in Samaria has been thirsty for a long time. She has tried unsuccessfully to quench this thirst through the relationships she has formed along the way. At the community well Jesus introduces her to the life-giving water that will be poured into all by the Holy Spirit.

The conversation they share is one that Jesus longs to have with each of us. If we really knew the gift God is offering to us, our grumbling and complaining would cease. Instead our prayer would constantly be "Sir, give me this water to drink!" Then our lives would be lived in a hope that looks forward to God's glory.

The Samaritan woman listens well to the words of Jesus and so discovers that God has never left his people. She experiences the presence of God in the man she meets at the well, and she has to immediately share him with the "thirsting" people of her town. Satiating this thirst becomes the foundation of her new life. Jesus teaches us through her that the sacrament of Holy Communion is not meant to feed us alone; it enables us to give the Lord the food of which the apostles did not know.

St. Thérèse also discovered that Holy Communion is the means by which God's hunger and thirst for the human family is satisfied. Jesus' words from the cross, "I thirst," opened her to a deeper awareness of the mystery of his sacrificial death. In turn she dedicated her life to quenching his thirst by allowing the love of God that was poured into her heart by the Holy Spirit to determine every facet of her life. She believed that the thirst of Christ is the source of charity in the human heart; it instilled within her a passion to bring as many souls as possible to him.

The cry of Jesus on the Cross sounded continually in my heart: "I thirst!" These words ignited within me an unknown and very living fire.

Sunday, Week Three, Cycle B
  First Reading: Exodus 20:1–17
  Second Reading: 1 Corinthians 1:22–25
  Gospel: John 2:13–25

Overturning the Obstacles

The words God speaks in the book of Exodus are pure gift. Although they are familiarly known as the Ten Commandments, they are much more than a list of what ought to be done and what ought to be avoided. Given as a sign of his covenant with the people, the words already betray how "the foolishness of God" is greater than human wisdom, as St. Paul tells us in the Second Reading.

It does seem strange that the Creator of all that exists would need to tell us how to conduct ourselves, especially when the behaviors condemned naturally destroy the peace and harmony of life in the family and in the community. The reason behind these commandments has everything to do with deepening our understanding of being human. God's wisdom is revealed in that he shows us how we possess within our minds and hearts an innate sense of what will bring about an experience of living together that is rich and fulfilling.

The Crucifixion of Christ will definitively substantiate the words from the book of Exodus. By his death on the cross, Jesus eliminates whatever obstacles we place in the way of living with and behaving toward one another as we know we should. The sign of the cross is far greater than any sign God has ever worked. Human wisdom could never establish a rule or guideline for human behavior that could approximate the standard revealed in the life, death, and Resurrection of Christ.

Jesus enters the temple area filled with the wisdom of God, which asserts itself through his interaction with the money changers and his words about the temple's destruction. This historical moment, like the commandments given through Moses, is meant to direct our attention inward, to our hearts. Once we know that Jesus is speaking about the temple of his body, his action bears on the present moments of our lives.

We should allow the Lord to overturn, uproot, and chase away whatever obstacles we have welcomed into the temple of our bodies. We should never be afraid of his driving out whatever prevents us from seeing Christ crucified and the madness of his love. Jesus knows what we have in us, just as the Father knew when he gave the Ten Commandments to his people.

Fasting enables us to peer within our hearts in order to see whatever may be getting in the way of our relationship with God. The sacrifices we make are like the whip Jesus made out of cord, giving us a tangible sense of the importance of being emptied of self in order to be filled with the presence of God.

When we love we experience the need of saying a thousand foolish things.

Sunday, Week Three, Cycle C
  First Reading: Exodus 3:1–8, 13–15
  Second Reading: 1 Corinthians 10:1–6, 10–12
  Gospel: Luke 13:1–9

Hungering Without Complaint

God is well aware of the suffering of his people, and Moses learns this in the most unexpected way. Having fled Egypt in fear of Pharaoh's wrath, Moses is asked to return in order to lead the people "into a good and spacious land." The God of Abraham, Isaac, and Jacob sends Moses on a mission that will utterly transform his life and eventually the lives of countless others.

Moses' encounter with God is beyond anything he has experienced but not unrelated to the desire for justice that caused him to flee into the desert. Standing before the burning bush, Moses begins to see his life and his relationship with God in an entirely new way. The God who speaks the unmentionable name understands relationships from a perspective not bound by time or circumstance. Here God begins an educational process that will culminate with the sending of his own Son to deliver humanity from the lust that leads to destruction.

All of us who have been baptized into Christ eat "the same spiritual food" and drink "the same spiritual drink" as those who followed Moses. The bodies of those who complained about the provisions God supplied littered the desert, because they failed to appreciate that being human transcends the mere appetites of the body. We should never complain that God, who did not spare his only Son, is unconcerned about our life situations and the difficulties, challenges, and suffering we face. We should constantly nourish ourselves on the food and drink he has given us in

Christ, the rock, so that we too will enter into and possess that "promised land" that is our common destiny.

Jesus knows how difficult it can be to walk toward a burning bush, to stand and accept the presence of God as it bursts into our lives. He tells the people that the key to everything is repentance, a willed turning toward God, which alone can satisfy the hunger and thirst we have to be whole. This turning demands that we fast from everything that ultimately leads to our destruction and accept all that the God of Abraham, Isaac, and Jacob offers us in the person of his Son.

St. Thérèse appreciated how the education that began with Moses continued with Christ. In him God teaches each one of us just what it means to be the man or woman he created us to be. Thérèse's willingness to give her life to God was the best response she could make to what Jesus was teaching her about herself. She accepted his invitation to be instructed in the truth of divine and human loving, expressing it in the unique conditions and circumstances of her life.

Without showing Himself, without making his voice heard, Jesus teaches me in secret.

Monday, Week Three
    First Reading: 2 Kings 5:1–15b
    Gospel: Luke 4:24–30

Knowing Hunger

Seeing the connection between going without and growing closer to God can be tricky. Like Naaman the Syrian, we may hunger for wholeness but fill ourselves on things that actually prevent it.

In order to be healed of his leprosy, Naaman needs to fast; that is, he needs to die to his own way of doing things and submit to God. A little girl, an Israelite captured in war, helps him do this. She knows "there is a prophet in Israel" and encourages her master to go to him.

In Samaria the prophet Elisha presents Naaman with the "diet" that will cleanse him. Regrettably, the waters of the Jordan are entirely distasteful. Naaman cannot see the connection between what he desires and what he has been told to do.

The people of Nazareth in Jesus' time are as fed up as was Naaman. They cannot recognize the prophet in their midst, because they are filled with judgments. Theirs is a kind of impious indigestion that makes them rise up and drive Jesus away. They consider him to be too ordinary, too familiar, and too bland. They do not savor his words; they bristle at them. When Jesus compares them to their ancestors, who were too full to feast on the good things of the Lord, they rebel.

Jesus returns to Nazareth because he genuinely cares for his townspeople and wants them to stop eating the sumptuous foods that feed self-righteousness. He comes to those he loves, offering a new way of determining what will sustain them. He recounts the story of Naaman the Syrian in order to free the people of Nazareth from their fixed ideas of who he is. They need to look outside the comfort of what is familiar in order to see what God is doing in their midst.

The "fast" proposed by Jesus frightens the people. What they have been feeding on keeps them from hungering and thirsting for God and from seeing how far they have moved away from him. Jesus comes to arouse their hunger for God.

That is why fasting is so important: It puts us back in touch with what ultimately matters. Every twinge of hunger should remind us of God. Every pang allows us to see not only our need but also the One who can satisfy it.

Fasting is an opportunity to reflect on the difference between what is sumptuous and what is sustaining. Through it we can see God's power revealed in the most ordinary ways—a bath, a simple meal, a suggestion to a friend, an act of kindness, a little child.

I am the smallest of creatures; I know my misery and my feebleness, but I also know how much noble and good hearts love to do good.

Tuesday, Week Three
  First Reading: Daniel 3:25, 34–35
  Gospel: Matthew 18:21–35

Fasting From Vengeance

The question Peter asks Jesus in today's Gospel shows that he is learning how genuine prayer fosters greater openness to others. It also shows the struggles we encounter when trying to live the way of Jesus. There are times when these struggles shape our interior conversation with him, much like the issue Peter raises. We need the Lord to show us the way by explaining boundaries and clarifying expectations. We need the Lord to continually challenge what we've learned and how we're living it.

Of everything Jesus taught, the admonition to "[forgive] your brother from your heart" is perhaps the most complex. The pain of injustice and the feelings evoked by being wronged touch the depths of our humanity. If not properly checked, the desire to right wrongs can lead to vengeance and retaliation. We need the Lord's guidance and help to love our neighbors and pray for our persecutors.

Jesus' story illustrates how feeding resentment makes forgiveness difficult. For the unmerciful servant, forgiveness from the heart is difficult to swallow. It demands acknowledging and accepting the gift of mercy he has received. Only this can push aside bitterness and resentment. When God's mercy reigns in us, we can acknowledge wrongdoing for what it is without becoming a slave to its effects.

Forgiveness from the heart does not overlook accountability, and it does not require that I let someone who has wronged me back into my life. Jesus doesn't expect me to open myself to repeated injury or ongoing injustices. But he does ask that I forgive, that I pray for those who hurt me and wish them well. Forgiveness from the heart is freeing, because the pain of the wrong no longer controls my life and no longer suffocates my relationship with God and neighbor.

The words of Azariah in the First Reading are fitting in terms of Peter's question. From the midst of a white-hot furnace he raises his voice, with no thought of the injury being done to him. His words are directed at the misdeeds of his people, which have "brought low" the nation. He knows that the greatest gift he can give the Lord is a "contrite heart and humble spirit."

Humility and hunger for God are synonymous. Azariah is hungry to have God "bring glory to [his] name." He hungers for his people to be restored, to once again have a "prince, prophet, or leader" and a "place to offer first fruits, to find favor." He cries out to God, knowing that God will never forget him, "for those who trust in you cannot be put to shame."

Azariah was hungry, not for his own freedom but for the salvation of his people. Peter was hungry to learn just how to live his new life in Christ. Jesus is hungry to educate us about the essence of our humanity. Our hunger can put us in touch with God.

Oh how happy I am to see myself imperfect and to be in need of God's mercy.

Wednesday, Week Three
First Reading: Deuteronomy 4:1, 5–9
Gospel: Matthew 5:17–19

Fasting From Distractions

During Lent the Church wants us to be hungry. The purpose isn't to fill our minds with thoughts of food but to fill them with thoughts of God. Our physical condition often impacts our conversation with God.

Moses is aware of how easily the mind drifts to thoughts other than God. He knows that once the people "enter in and take possession of the land," they might forget how hungry they were to reach it. He sets before them the statutes and decrees he has received from God. From that point on every aspect of their lives will be subject to a law. The purpose is to remind them that they are God's people and that he is close to them "whenever [they] call upon him." The discipline of the Law enabled the people of Israel to live rightly.

Jesus takes up this same theme in his private conversation with the disciples. He comes not "to abolish the law or the prophets" but to renew them by the definitive interpretation he gives them. What God has done for no other nation, he has now done for all nations in Jesus his Son. As a result, greatness in the kingdom of God will no longer depend upon living the precepts of the Mosaic Law. It will now consist in living according to the mind of Christ.

While upholding the dignity of the Law and the prophets, Jesus' words help us grasp the purpose of our fasting. Like the statutes and decrees recalled in the First Reading, fasting is meant to remind us of who we are and to whom we belong. We fast for God and not ourselves.

We must therefore be constantly on our guard that what Christ has taught never slips from our memory. Memory opens us to the truth, and it binds us to Christ. Jesus fulfills the aim of the Law and illuminates its essential character, so that "the smallest letter" and "the smallest part of a letter" will help us adhere to him, until "all things have taken place."

Fasting can seem like "the smallest" part of our spiritual life, but what we do with our bodies impacts our souls. Sacrifice gives us an opportunity to strengthen the ties that bind us to the mind of Christ and strengthen our allegiance to the truth. We abstain from thoughts of self-sufficiency and self-importance, which cloud our memory of the truth. This is the little way, and it is never insignificant, for it conforms us to the Law, the prophets, and the mind of Christ.

When we act according to nature, it is impossible for the soul being corrected to understand her faults.

Thursday, Week Three
First Reading: Jeremiah 7:23–28
Gospel: Luke 11:14–23

Empty Mouths

The end of the First Reading is a great introduction to the Gospel. The people of Israel have "walked in the hardness of their evil hearts," no longer listening or paying attention to God. They refuse to take correction, and so God laments, "Faithfulness has disappeared; the word itself is banished from their speech."

The Gospel begins with Jesus casting out a demon that is mute. The man unable to speak bears a physical sign of the condition described by Jeremiah. Instead of lamenting the man's situation, Jesus proves himself the antidote. He loosens the man's tongue, enabling him to speak of God's faithfulness.

The people who witness the exorcism seem to have stopped listening to God. They, like the people of Nazareth, are unable to see the prophet in front of them. Once again there is a demand for a "sign from heaven." Some even think that Jesus is in league with the devil.

The reaction of the people to the action of God shows just how desperately they need to turn back to him. The hardness of their hearts must yield to bended knee. "Come,… let us kneel before the LORD who made us," the Responsorial Psalm urges (Psalm 95). The people's physical posture must be an honest indication of the contrition in their hearts. Only this can open them to the tenderness and compassion of God. Only this will free their mouths to sing God's praises.

It's true that the season of Lent can pass us by without our ever bending our wills. The refusal to fast, for example, is a cheap disguise for a refusal to bow. We can either gather with Jesus and follow the way marked out for us or distance ourselves and scatter. The choice is always ours. If we participate in the lenten practices as best we can, then we will surely know at its conclusion that "the Kingdom of God has come upon" us.

When Jesus casts out the demon that is mute, the observers prove just how overweight they are. They are so bloated in their own self-importance that they fail to recognize the food that Christ offers. Jesus is patient with them. His words call them to fast from everything that is inconsequential. He wants them with him and not against him. This requires one thing: that they listen to God.

This dramatic passage should caution us against becoming caught up in the insignificant. Jesus has the power to drive out of our lives anything that prevents us from rejoicing in God and giving him thanks. And because some demons can be driven out only by prayer and fasting, we should willingly undertake everything the Church asks us to do throughout these forty days.

How great is the power of Prayer! One could call it a Queen who has at each instant free access to the King and who is able to obtain whatever she asks.

Friday, Week Three
   First Reading: Hosea 14:2–10
   Gospel: Mark 12:28–34

The Two as One

The scribe who comes to Jesus is "not far from the Kingdom of God." He has grasped the fact that love of God and love of neighbor can never be separated. He comes to Jesus with an understanding of the truth that ends up silencing everyone in attendance. His question cuts to the heart of what it means to be a follower of Christ and a child of God.

The reading from Hosea offers a beautiful description of this. Those who return to God asking forgiveness for iniquities will be healed. God's love will be given freely to them, and they will be spared his wrath. God will be "like the dew" for them, and they will "blossom like the lily." There is great comfort in knowing that because of God we will bear fruit!

If we have stumbled, the prophet's words should help us stand. Consequently we should feed on them, even as we persist in our fast. They should satisfy our appetite for understanding the reasons for fasting and abstinence, penance and self-denial. We should let the lush and vivid imagery soak in, just as it surely did in the mind and heart of the scribe. His words to Jesus unquestionably flow from his own experience of being freely loved by God. He has been fed "with the best of wheat, / and with honey from the rock," as the Responsorial Psalm says (Psalm 81:17), because he has listened well to the voice of God.

Fasting trains our ears to listen better to God. It doesn't eliminate distractions but helps us order them rightly. All too often we waste time trying to put aside the thoughts that intrude upon our conversation with God. In wrestling with them we turn from God. Fasting reminds us of our weakness, which in turn prompts us to bring everything to God, including whatever encroaches upon the mind during prayer—any chore, any pain, any struggle, any hope. Instead of fighting to control a distraction, we should surrender it to God. After all, prayer is not the time for telling God who he is; it is the time in which God tells us who we are.

In today's Gospel it isn't Jesus who passes a test; it is the scribe. He leaves with a greater sense of self. He has stood firm and with prudence walked the paths of the LORD. He has learned what means more to God than burnt offering and sacrifices.

All this, however, does not prevent both distractions and sleepiness from visiting me, but at the end of the thanksgiving when I see that I've made it badly I make a resolution to be thankful all through the rest of the day.

Saturday, Week Three
First Reading: Hosea 6:1–6
Gospel: Luke 18:9–14

Fed Up

The tax collector who figures prominently in today's Gospel is surely familiar with the words of the prophet Hosea. He may have spent his days trading in earthly currency, but he has spent his time in the temple trading in something more valuable: the mercy of God. He demonstrates a confidence at odds with his social standing. Although reluctant to lift his head, he knows that he can lift his heart.

This man is empty and hungry. He comes to the temple hoping to be fed. He knows that he feeds his life on other things, but he also knows what alone will satisfy him. His hunger doesn't cause him to judge, condemn, or despise others; his hunger drives him to the temple and brings him to his knees.

The Pharisee in the story has forgotten the stirring words of the prophet Hosea. He comes to the temple satisfied, thinking his personal accomplishments will win him favor with God. He leaves the temple exactly as he entered, for his piety is "like the dew that early passes away."

The self-righteous, to whom the parable is told, are too well fed to grasp what Jesus is saying. Like the Pharisee in the story, they feast on their own moral and spiritual perfection and social standing. They have gorged themselves on judging, condemning, and despising others. They may feel justified in lifting their heads to heaven, but their souls are weighed down by the works of their own hands. They have eaten so much that they have no room to feast on the mercy of God.

Fasting has nothing whatsoever to do with showing God what we can accomplish. Fasting is aimed at bringing us "to the temple" with a heart that hungers for wholeness. It is meant to engender within us the plaintive cry for mercy that leads to justification. Fasting is meant to reacquaint us with our innate appreciation of what is ultimately of lasting worth. Fasting helps us leave our "tax collecting" in order to trade in that which is priceless and of lasting value.

Condemning others is easy; seeing ourselves as we are is more difficult. Those who have listened well to the words of the prophet Hosea, those who have listened well to the parable Jesus speaks to the self-righteous, are unafraid of seeing themselves. They know that God isn't pleased with burnt offerings but with the offering of a contrite heart. Their hunger from fasting drives them to the temple, and they leave satisfied.

In order that this judgment be favorable or rather that I be not judged at all, I want to be charitable in my thoughts towards others at all times, for Jesus has said: "Judge not, and you shall not be judged."

Week Four

Many souls say: I don't have the strength to accomplish this sacrifice. Let them do, then, what I did: exert a great effort. God never refuses that first grace that gives one the courage to act; afterwards, the heart is strengthened and one advances from victory to victory.

Sunday, Week Four, Cycle A
  First Reading: 1 Samuel 16:1b, 6–7, 10–13a
  Second Reading: Ephesians 5:8–14
  Gospel: John 9:1–41

Seeing in the Light

God's words to Samuel are as true for us as they were in the selection of David as Israel's king: "Not as man sees does God see." God does not judge according to our appearance but according to our hearts. His gaze penetrates into the depths of who we truly are, seeing everything there, even what our parents may not recognize.

In a sense all of us are "blind from birth" to the truth of our humanity. The grace that comes to us in Christ allows us to discover what the Lord wants of us, permitting the works of God to be uniquely displayed in the actual conditions and circumstances of our lives.

The Pharisees whom Jesus encounters refuse to welcome the light that brings us out of darkness. Their sin remains because of the narrowness of vision with which they look at the world. Their superficial gaze prevents them from seeing the hand of God at work in the life of the man brought before them. Their limited perception extends even to their understanding of the Sabbath.

The Pharisees threaten to expel from the synagogue the man born blind and anyone else who acknowledges that Jesus is the Christ. They remain in their sin because they are blind to the currency Jesus uses to carry out the work of the One who sent him. Jesus has come to purchase wholeness of life for those willing to accept all that God sees in them.

Just as the man who washes in the Pool of Siloam didn't ask to be healed, many of us didn't ask to be baptized. Through the loving and attentive care of Jesus' disciples, whether our parents or others, our condition was brought to the attention of Christ, and we were washed clean. Like David we were anointed, and from that day on "the spirit of the LORD" rushed upon us. The light that came into our lives that day exposed "the fruitless works of darkness" so that we could grow in "goodness and righteousness and truth." However, remaining in the light requires the willingness to trade our lives on the same currency with which Jesus purchased our salvation.

St. Thérèse was able to accept what God saw within her. Thinking of herself as little, as insignificant as David was in the eyes of Jesse and Samuel, did not restrict the way she lived her vocation. As a matter of fact, it instilled a tremendous sense of confidence and hope regarding the effectiveness of God's love within the circumstances of her life. The light of Christ shone upon her, and the progression of her sight continued up to the moment of her death. St. Thérèse allowed everything to come into the light of Christ, and thus she became a light that continues to shine upon the whole world.

It was He who taught me that science hidden from the wise and the prudent and revealed to little ones.

Sunday, Week Four, Cycle B
  First Reading: 2 Chronicles 36:14–16, 19–23
  Second Reading: Ephesians 2:4–10
  Gospel: John 3:14–21

A Place in Heaven

The opening paragraph of the passage from the second book of Chronicles presents a frightening picture. Israel despised God's word, ridiculed his messengers, and laughed at his prophets. The people pushed God so completely from their lives "that there was no remedy." Having given up on God, the people saw their temple burned and the walls of Jerusalem demolished. Many were slain by enemies, and the survivors came to be ruled by a foreign king, Nebuchadnezzar.

Fortunately God never stops loving or caring for his people. He patiently waited for a time when the consequences of their actions would make them once again receptive to his providential care. Long before the events described came to pass, hope came in the words of the prophet Jeremiah. Desolation was not the final word in God's relationship with his people. The events of history, after seventy years had passed, would prove God's relentless commitment to prevent his people's eternal loss in the impenetrable darkness caused by sin.

The words Jesus speaks to Nicodemus verify that God is never eager to condemn the human family. The signs within the events of history have always revealed God's love and pointed to his commitment to his people. That's why Jesus connects his life to that of the raising of the serpent in the desert. He wants us to understand that his self-sacrifice is in continuity with the past.

Through his flesh and blood, Jesus will definitively express the generosity of God's mercy.

It is important to remember that God sent his Son into the world as the ultimate remedy for the obstinacy cultivated by human autonomy. The paschal mystery is richer in hope than the words of Jeremiah. We know that God has accomplished everything in Christ, that there is no need to wait for something more.

The condemned are those who refuse to accept what God has given in the richness of grace that flows from his Son; thus condemnation is something one brings upon oneself. God's riches can never be exhausted; they are not earned and are not merited. It is only "by grace" that we "have been saved," and by accepting God's love we are free to live the good life that from the beginning he meant us to live.

St. Thérèse knew that the whole of the Christian life is meant to be an ever-expanding experience of our humanity from the perspective of God's favor. Being a Christian is as easy as accepting God's love. As Thérèse grew in faith, she came to understand that the only way to be fully alive is to acknowledge that even now we are united with Christ. This truth instilled a confident hope for which she never took credit but that she eagerly shared with the novices she trained, with the sisters with whom she lived, and through her writings, with the entire world.

I believed, I felt there was a heaven and that this heaven is peopled with souls who actually love me, who consider me their child.

Sunday, Week Four, Cycle C
  First Reading: Joshua 5:9, 10–12
  Second Reading: 2 Corinthians 5:17–21
  Gospel: Luke 15:1–3, 11–32

Eating on Our Own

The Gospel parable not only emphasizes God's unconditional love but also describes salvation history. The decision of Adam and Eve to have a "share of [the] estate" moved humanity away from God. In a sense we found ourselves in a strange land, for we, like the younger son, journeyed far from our true home and Father. Over the course of time, we squandered our inheritance through the reduction of human life to the merely physical. Natural urges and corporeal drives overwhelmed and suppressed the desires of the human spirit. As the heart turned to stone, we lost a sense of home and the truth of who we are.

The difference between our situation and that of the young man in Jesus' story is that our Father couldn't wait to have us come to our senses. The filth and squalor of our fallen condition moved him to send his Son, our brother, to bring us home. In the share of the estate belonging to Jesus, already "God was reconciling the world to himself."

The response to human autonomy was the willing submission of our brother. He left home to bring us the message that God does not hold our faults against us. Through his willingness to become sin, Jesus opens us to the goodness of God.

The Father's hope that we return is expressed in the way he made it possible for us to become "a new creation." In our reunion with the Father, we are not slaves! The shame of our former condition is taken away. Like the father who welcomed home his profligate son, God welcomes each one of us in Christ. He places upon us the robe of salvation and prepares a banquet not made by human hands.

Jesus welcomes sinners and eats with them because he sees them as his brothers and sisters. He wants to free the human heart from its rough confinement in order to be reconciled with God.

It is no surprise that the self-righteous cannot understand this. They are like the older brother in the story of the Prodigal Son: They have forgotten who their Father is. They have remained "at home," but their hearts are distant.

St. Thérèse never forgot whose child she was. While her own parents were sources of blessing and examples of holiness, she knew that her ultimate Father was God. She was happy to be welcomed home, led there by Christ, and she rejoiced to wear the robe, put on the ring, and feast at God's table.

It is upon heaven that everything hinges.

Monday, Week Four
  First Reading: Isaiah 65:17–21
  Gospel: John 4:43–54

The Hunger Pangs of Suffering
Today the words the prophet Isaiah speaks on behalf of God are a fitting response to the fatigue generated by a true fast. Sounds of crying and weeping are natural outcomes of limiting our food and drink during Lent. Isaiah's words do not ridicule our frustrations and complaints.

The prophet paints a picture of what happens when people allow God to rescue them. Those who let God help them will know "rejoicing and happiness." The disciplines of Lent should move us closer to the God who longs to "create Jerusalem to be a joy / and its people to be a delight."

After feasting with those who have seen what he can do, Jesus returns to Cana. Here in the place "where he had made the water wine," Jesus reveals exactly what the new heavens and the new earth will resemble. Cana is a fitting place for this, because Jesus' response to the couple's need for wine was a sign that through his blood he would end humanity's long fast from the inebriation of divinity.

The fast we see in today's Gospel is caused by the illness of a loved one. The official craves his son's return to health. Although he is not a Jew, living in Cana has made him aware of Jesus. He reasons that if this man can change water to wine, he can change illness into well-being.

The intense appetite of the royal official pushes him to do whatever it takes to have his son made whole. In his hunger is revealed the real purpose of our lenten sacrifices. They should compel us toward Christ as the source of everything we need in this life.

Initially Jesus responds to the royal official as he has to others who were seeking a sign. He seems frustrated by the request, but this is for the man's own benefit. Jesus wants the official to know that his faith, his confidence in Jesus, has healed his son. When Jesus dismisses the royal official, it is with a guarantee that the boy will live.

Too often we grow weary of fasting because it seems to have little or no effect. The attitude of the official in this story should put an end to our expectations. The location of the story reminds us that we have the greatest of all gifts in the chalice offered each Sunday. In the cup is the blood of everlasting life.

Cana was the place of miracles back then; the Mass is the place of miracles now. Fasting before we receive the Eucharist helps us rid ourselves of expectations, moving us to trust that whatever God tells us to do is exactly what is needed.

God cannot inspire unrealizable desires. I can then, in spite of my littleness, aspire to holiness.

Tuesday, Week Four
First Reading: Ezekiel 47:1–9, 12
Gospel: John 5:1–16

The Hunger That Brings Wholeness

In the vision of Ezekiel, we hear a prophetic word about the temple not made by human hands (see John 2:18–22). The life-giving waters that flow from "beneath the threshold of the temple" signify the water that comes from the temple of Christ's body. This water will refresh and renew all who drink it.

Yet, as the Gospel passage shows, in order to drink from the streams of everlasting life, we have to get to the water. Like the father in yesterday's Gospel, the Samaritan woman at the well, and the tax collector in the temple, we have to come to God. This will require the most difficult of all fasts, because in order to reach God we must stop being victims. We have to stop coming up with excuses about why we haven't made our way to the pool.

The paralyzed man in today's Gospel has been lying around for thirty-eight years waiting for something to happen. He has been living on a diet of "woe is me." He has become so settled in his victimhood that his response to Jesus is one extended justification for being right where he is. Instead of pleading to be healed, he offers Christ the insignificant morsels on which he's been feeding his self-pity.

This man, more paralyzed in spirit than in body, needs to be refreshed by the waters "that gladden the city of God," of which today's Responsorial Psalm speaks (Psalm 46:5). He need not fear, for the Lord of hosts is with him. Jesus raises him up and sends him on his way as a sign of the astounding things he has come to do on the earth.

The man leaves, taking with him the sign of his former infirmity, only to be questioned about his condition. His healing now becomes an occasion for Jesus to educate about the meaning of the Sabbath.

The God of Jacob has sent his Son into the world to free us from the paralysis of sin and the emotional malaise that comes from our original wound. Through the sacrifice of Christ, God makes us well and tells us to "not sin any more." Instead of lamenting our weak, frail, and vulnerable condition, we should stand up! Christ sends us into the world as signs that God alone is the refuge and strength of the human family.

The evidence we carry of our former condition is meant to be a reminder of the good work God has begun in us, not of our victimhood. Through, with, and in Christ, we can stand like a tree planted beside the life-giving waters that flow from the sanctuary. There our "fruit shall serve for food" and our "leaves for medicine."

Yes, the little flower was going to be born again to life, and the luminous Ray that had warmed her again was not to stop its favors.

Wednesday, Week Four
  First Reading: Isaiah 49:8–15
  Gospel: John 5:17–30

Fasting Through the Hour

Jesus describes in his own way the favorable time spoken about in the First Reading. He is appointed by the Father as the "covenant to the people." He has the power to say to prisoners, "Come out!", and to those who are in darkness, "Show yourselves!" Jesus has come to lead and guide us to a place where scorching wind and sun will never plague us, to springs of water where we will never again be hungry and thirsty.

At the sound of Jesus' voice, the dead will leave their graves, and those who did good will rise again to life. What the account of judgment in today's Gospel lacks in spectacular imagery, it makes up for in its emphasis on the unity of the Father and Son. Jesus has come to a moment in his ministry when it is time to push aside any confusion about the purpose of his coming and the nature of his identity.

This solemn moment in which Jesus speaks openly about himself should cause those who make contrary claims to choke on their words. The Son of Man comes into the world with the sole aim of doing the "will of the one who sent [him]." To suggest that he is confused or uncertain concerning the Father's will is an attempt to make him our equal.

Jesus knows why the Father has sent him, in terms of both his humanity and his divinity. He knows well the words of the prophet Isaiah, and he makes those words uniquely his own. Isaiah entrusted them to the memory of God's people in order that, when the solemn hour came, they would recognize the one standing before them.

How sad it is that, in hearing the words of today's Gospel, many want to lessen their impact and empty them of meaning. Every tendency to treat Jesus like an itinerant preacher or perplexed holy man should be coughed up and spit out. When the king of the Ninevites heard the preaching of Jonah, he repented. When we hear the words Jesus speaks in today's Gospel, we should repent as well. Emboldened by our fasting, we should turn wholeheartedly to the Lord and call on him from our hearts. We should earnestly put away the childish thoughts that distance us from Christ.

Jesus is proof that God never abandons or forgets his people. As the source of life, Jesus extends to us the love and compassion of the Father. His words are solemn but not somber, for they raise us up when we have fallen and support us as we follow after him. Listening as he explains himself to the Jews should fill us with songs of gladness.

Lent is one extended hour in which the Son stands before us, offering life to anyone he chooses. If we have emptied ourselves through a faithful and disciplined fast, then we are ready to eat all that he sets before us.

It seems to me that when Jesus descends into my heart He is content to find Himself so well received and I, too, am content.

Thursday, Week Four
  First Reading: Exodus 37:7–14
  Gospel: John 5:31–47

The Taste of Egypt
In the First Reading we see how easy it is to return to that which is insubstantial and unfulfilling. God had been caring for the Israelites since bringing them "out of the land of Egypt," providing food and water, protection, and even healing for their transgressions. While Moses was away, the people turned from God and gorged themselves on lascivious idols, "making for themselves a molten calf and worshiping it." Truly they were a stiff-necked people, because the taste of Egypt lingered.

The Israelites failed to realize that Moses hadn't left them. He went up Mount Sinai in order to bring back to them the tablets of the Law. His time on the mountain was spent with God, who put in stone the expansiveness of his care and the impenetrable boundaries of his commitment to them. The commandments do not bind or restrict human life; they safeguard it. They illuminate what's possible when we allow ourselves to be fed by no other god than the Lord Almighty.

The people in today's Gospel no longer have the Word of God in them. Like the Israelites in the desert, they have abandoned the way pointed out by God. They have fashioned the Scriptures into a lifeless idol. They have forgotten the Truth whom Moses served and to which John testified. They are too stiff-necked to accept the words of Jesus or the works that testify on his behalf. They claim they have placed their hope in Moses, not realizing that Moses is accusing them before the Father.

Jesus' words resonate with the frustration voiced in the First Reading. The people must once again be confronted with God's blazing wrath in order to fully understand how he "relented in the punishment he had threatened." The people cannot come to Jesus and have life until they see that he stands in the breach between them and God. Jesus' discourse aims at helping them acknowledge their misdeeds so that he can wipe those misdeeds from before their eyes.

Fasting and abstaining with the community challenge our autonomy and bend our wills. These practices are meant to shatter the idols we have erected and replace them with Christ. They aim at helping us to go to him "to have life." Fasting and abstaining, our spiritual diet, cleanse us and prompt a hunger for virtue.

The words Jesus speaks in today's Gospel reveal the consistency of God's plan. The God who longs for us, the God who reached out in friendship to Abraham, the God who formed a tribe and a nation, has always provided for the needs of his people. In the flesh and blood of his Son, he now provides for us in an unimaginable way.

When we willingly fast we sustain our hunger for the living bread come down from heaven. Only then can we begin to grasp the Father's testimony on behalf of his Son.

You desire to nourish me with Your divine substance and yet I am a poor little thing who would return to nothingness if Your divine glance did not give me life from one moment to the next.

Friday, Week Four
  First Reading: Wisdom 2:1a, 12–22
  Gospel: John 7:1–2, 10, 25–30

Taking Refuge

As we move closer to the end of Lent, the Scriptures begin preparing us for the events of Holy Week. In the First Reading today, we learn that the method of the wicked is "revilement and torture." They intentionally seek the destruction and death of the just, in a vain attempt to prove that God will not save the righteous. They follow their own paths because they have lost all knowledge of God.

The words of the wicked are a frightening depiction of evil. The wicked intentionally cause pain and seek the destruction of the innocent, blinded by the desire to tear down the trust and confidence that make one a child of God. They cannot see the innocent soul's reward, because holiness is "obnoxious" to them, and "knowledge of God" a hardship.

The portrayal of the wicked underscores two errors in judgment that commonly threaten our relationship with God. The first sees horrible, senseless tragedies as signs that God doesn't care about the human family, that we are on our own. This is simply a way of judging God according to human standards, an excuse to follow one's own paths.

The second error is feeling threatened or judged by the righteousness of others. If we find the goodness of our neighbor to be distasteful, then we have probably lost our hunger for God. The holiness of our neighbors is not an affront to our own efforts at loving God. In fact, it can give us hope that we too can grow in virtue and be one with God. And rejoicing in the good fortune of others is an expression of genuine love.

Fasting helps cleanse the palate of the aftertaste of wicked judgments. Through our simple lenten diet, we regain our taste for holiness and the good things of God. Self-denial bends the will toward God and lets us see that he is always "close to the brokenhearted," as the Responsorial Psalm says (Psalm 34:19). Our spirits can be crushed by our own imperfections and sins, but God seeks always to revive them.

Jesus, familiar with the ways of the wicked, takes refuge for a while from Judea, where the Jews are trying to kill him. For us there is no better protection from the willed destructive tendencies of man than fasting. Those who seek sanctuary in fasting can rid themselves of the dark elements of the human condition.

Jesus doesn't remain in hiding but emerges to confront the bloated ideas people have of him. They think they know who he is and where he is from, but they feed only on the physical, the historical, the chronological; on what they can see, touch, control, and manipulate. They will put him to the test, and Jesus in turn will show them that God "watches over all his bones" and will deliver him from all his troubles.

If only you knew what goes on! How little it takes to lose control of oneself!

Saturday, Week Four
   First Reading: Jeremiah 11:18–20
   Gospel: John 7:40–53

Going Without
Ever since God spared the life of Isaac, the Jews had been look-ing for the lamb of sacrifice. Far from heeding Jeremiah's words, they led the prophet away "like a trusting lamb led to slaughter." Jeremiah took refuge in the Lord. He expressed a passionate long-ing for "the Lamb of God who takes away the sin of the world" (John 1:29) and who will restore humanity to the splendor of the beginning of creation.

   The Pharisees in today's Gospel are as blind as the people who hatched their plot against Jeremiah. As the crowd becomes more convinced that Jesus is a prophet, the Pharisees refuse to recog-nize the Lamb in their midst. They are so full of misconceptions about the identity of the Messiah that they cannot see in the words and works of Christ the presence of the God of Abraham, Isaac, and Jacob.

   The fast that would be good for these Pharisees is a fast from trying to be in control: control of the crowd, of Jesus' fate, and of God's plan. Fasting and abstinence are means of relinquishing control. Although this may be through simple means—no meat, sugar, soda, or coffee—it always has effect.

   The crowd surrounding Jesus may be divided about whether he is a prophet or the Christ, but they are in agreement about the way he speaks. They have never before heard anyone speak like him, which makes them take notice. This distresses the Pharisees; they are losing the upper hand. Thus they condemn the crowd.

Through the Church Jesus continues to speak in a way unlike any other. To hear his words we must let go of our misconceptions about what God should be doing and how our lives should be. We need to stop trying to force Jesus into acceptable categories that strip him of his divinity or of his humanity. We must not condemn him for what we think he has failed to do but be assumed into what he has already accomplished.

Control is difficult to relinquish. The ideas, attitudes, and actions on which we base our lives can deceive us about the truth of our humanity. Jesus, because he comes from God, can never deceive us. His death and resurrection are the answer to Jeremiah's prayer for vengeance. God does not destroy those who hatch a plot against his Son: He lets his Son be slaughtered, but this is how he saves the sinner who comes to him.

Those who fast find that relinquishing control gets easier. Every day that I can say no to myself and bend my will out of love for God makes trusting him easier. This is true for every believer, from the youngest child to the pope in Rome.

You know yourself that those souls are rare who don't measure the divine power according to their own narrow minds.

WEEK FIVE

During the course of the whole trip, we were lodged in princely hotels; never had I been surrounded with so much luxury. There's no mistake about it: riches don't bring happiness…. Ah! I really felt it: joy isn't found in the material objects surrounding us but in the inner recesses of the soul. One can possess joy in a prison cell as well as in a palace.

Sunday, Week Five, Cycle A
   First Reading: Ezekiel 37:12–14
   Second Reading: Romans 8:8–11
   Gospel: John 11:1–45

"Come Out!"

St. Paul reminds us that if the spirit of God has made his home in us, then we can be certain that our own "mortal bodies" will have life through that spirit. Even though "the body is dead because of sin," sin is not the final word. Just as he did for Lazarus, Jesus will cry, "Come out," and he "will open [our] graves and have [us] rise from them." The final word we will hear is from the one who loves us, just as he loved Martha, Mary, and their brother. When the spirit of the Lord lives in us, sin ends not in death but in God's glory.

Jesus therefore returns to Bethany with the same purposefulness with which he emerged from the temptations in the desert to undertake his public ministry. He has come back so that his own disciples may believe and receive the light. He has returned to Bethany so that we can appreciate what it means to return to the Father.

Jesus is not afraid of being stoned; his interest lies exclusively in the spiritual. He can even take time in returning, because Lazarus is only resting.

Like Martha and Mary, we weep and bemoan our circumstances, thinking if only the Lord had been here, things would be different. Our preoccupation with the unspiritual prevents us from truly believing that God will give Jesus whatever he asks.

We may believe with Martha in the resurrection on the last day, but Jesus is in Bethany for something more immediate. He brings the very power of God into the present situation of loss and grief. In doing so he makes it clear that he is exactly what Martha hopes for. When Lazarus steps out into the light, Martha gains an entirely new appreciation of just what it means that Jesus is the Christ, the one who has come into the world. And Mary, who threw herself at the feet of Christ in debilitating sorrow, from this point on will throw herself at his feet in humble adoration.

Every moment of Jesus' public ministry, everything he says and does, points toward his death on the cross and his own time in the tomb. Only through his paschal mystery can we appreciate why he weeps, heals, forgives, and encourages others. Only through his paschal mystery can we appreciate what it means that he is Lord.

The paschal mystery is also the key to understanding the life of a cloistered nun. The grille separating her from the world is like the stone rolled before the tomb of Lazarus. And the woman entombed in the cloister is not dead or even resting but alive! The Spirit has given life to her mortal body; he has unbound her to let her go free.

Did he not allow Lazarus to die even after Martha and Mary told Him he was sick?

Sunday, Week Five, Cycle B
  First Reading: Jeremiah 31:31–34
  Second Reading: Hebrews 5:7–9
  Gospel: John 12:20–33

"Not for My Sake But for Yours"

In today's Gospel some Greeks approach Philip with a request to see Jesus. Their life outside the covenant means they have little knowledge of God's relentless and unyielding care for his people. Nonetheless, Jesus has awakened in them what is presented in the book of Jeremiah, the law that God has planted deep within every human heart. Their request of Philip demonstrates how the new covenant will be distinguished by its inclusiveness, by the fact that it is for all women and men. Through the gift of his Son, we have become God's friends (see John 15:15). This is precisely how the prince of this world is overthrown.

"The hour…for the Son of Man to be glorified" is the hour in which we recognize what God has done for us. The new covenant promised in the First Reading aims at the forgiveness of our iniquity in the nearly incomprehensible way of God, who will not remember our sin. This recognition alone truly leads us to "hate [our lives] in this world" so that we can follow Christ. We come to hate whatever encourages us to think and act for ourselves alone. We humbly submit to Christ, knowing that our lives united with his can become "source[s] of eternal salvation" for our neighbors.

Jesus reminds us that the voice from heaven speaks to and for all of us. He has no need to hear the Father's voice, even though his heart is troubled. His honor is to serve the Father, having "learned obedience from what he suffered." This education began the moment Jesus was conceived in Mary's womb. Love moved him to empty himself of divinity and become one like us in all things but sin.

The suffering that troubles Jesus' heart is not the physical pain he will endure on the cross; rather it is the knowledge that some people will not accept God's love. He longs to set free the law that is written in all our hearts. Yet Jesus knows this can only happen if "a grain of wheat falls to the ground and dies," so he accepts the reason that he has come to this hour.

In the quiet confines of a Carmelite cloister, a young woman discovered the sentence passed on the world the day that Jesus died. This discovery led her to see her own small, limited, and insignificant life in a positive way and to hear the voice of the Father for herself. This compelled her to find the most fitting means of giving thanks to God for the prayers, entreaties and silent tears that were the source of her salvation.

What an abundant harvest you have reaped. You have sown in tears, but soon you will see the result of your works, you will return filled with joy, carrying sheaves in your arms.

Sunday, Week Five, Cycle C
   First Reading: Isaiah 43:16–21
   Second Reading: Philippians 3:8–14
   Gospel: John 8:1–11

Knowing Christ

Each of the readings for this Sunday should draw our attention to what lies ahead—the events of Holy Week.

St. Paul reminds us on our lenten journey that nothing can outweigh "the supreme good of knowing Christ Jesus." We try no longer for perfection by our own efforts but content ourselves with the perfection that comes through faith. Our only desire should be "to know him and the power of his resurrection." Like St. Paul we must be prepared to be captured by Christ in the events of Holy Week.

The power of Holy Week is also portrayed in today's Gospel. After the crowd has formed and the adulterous woman is brought forward, Jesus bends down and writes in the sand. He does not question the woman's past, for there is no need to recall the past. Jesus has come to make "a way in the sea / and a path in the mighty waters." His singular concern is for everyone gathered around him, all of them sinners, to set out on this path. He wants them to look forward to the salvation that awaits them, to that moment when he will say to each, "Has no one condemned you?" The crowd disperses in the same way as should our past once we have been captured by Christ.

The words "go, and from now on do not sin any more" enabled St. Paul to "[strain] forward to what lies ahead." Far from thinking he had already won "the prize of God's upward calling in Christ," St. Paul knew that the only thing that mattered was that he had a place in Christ. He had not yet become perfect, but he longed to share in Christ's sufferings "by being conformed to his death."

It wasn't that St. Paul hoped to be crucified. What he hoped was that he would expend his life in sacrificial loving. He counted all else as rubbish. In the face of love, nothing else matters.

The words of St. Paul help us understand why St. Thérèse looked so fervently for a vocation within a vocation, why she wanted to repay the Lord for his goodness to her. The zeal of Paul's words could only come from someone passionately in love with Christ. This passion resonated with Thérèse's and opened her to the possibility of translating her love for Christ into every prayer, every gesture, every chore, and every command of religious life. All she wanted was to know Christ more and more. Love became the means of acquiring this knowledge.

It is the little crosses that are our whole joy; they are more common than big ones and prepare the heart to receive the latter when this is the will of our good Master.

Monday, Week Five

First Reading: Daniel 13:1–9, 15–17, 19–30, 33–62

Gospel, Cycles A and B: John 8:1–11

(see commentary for Sunday, Week Five, Cycle C)

Gospel, Cycle C: John 8:12–20

Where Are We Going?

For Christians, forgetting where we are going is the same as forgetting who we are. When we forget that our destiny is to be forever with God, we can forget that "we are God's children now" (1 John 3:2).

The men in today's First Reading have forgotten they are sons of Israel. They can no longer see beyond the immediacy of their own situation. If only they could recall the God of their ancestors, the God who guides his people along right paths and is true to his name, then they would not bring a false accusation against Susanna.

God has prepared a banquet for all of us, and so his spirit moves the heart of Daniel to bring to light the wicked deeds of the old men. The revelation frees Susanna from the unjust condemnation and brings upon the old men the same sentence they sought to impose on her. It also reorients the people's perspective toward their true hope: dwelling forever in the Lord's own house. It reminds them of who they are.

In today's Gospel Jesus gives testimony in the temple treasury on his own behalf. This upsets the Pharisees, because they too have forgotten who they are. They measure Jesus' worth according to human standards. Someone else must verify Jesus' testimony, they say, if his words are to be valid. While they seem open to believing, the obstacle to belief is of their own making.

Jesus admits to their accusation but asserts that he can speak on his own behalf because he never speaks alone. He and the Father are one; this truth enables him to speak words that free people from darkness. His claim to be the light of the world is rooted in the security of his identity: He knows who he is and where he is going. And he reminds us all of who we are and where we are going.

Knowing Jesus means knowing the Father. The security of our identity as sons and daughters of God is rooted in our relationship with Christ, which refreshes us and revives our drooping spirits. Through it we no longer walk in darkness but move toward our heavenly homeland, spending freely from the treasury of God's love.

The testimony we give is determined by the way we incarnate God's love. We do not do this on our own behalf: The Spirit has been poured into our hearts so that our judgments may be sound. When our identity is secure in our relationship with the Father and the Son, we can help lead others to the garden of eternal refuge and the banquet of everlasting delights.

I have no merit at all, then, in not having given myself up to the love of creatures. I was preserved from it only through God's mercy!

Tuesday, Week Five
First Reading: Numbers 21:4–9
Gospel: John 8:21–30

That Which Is Above

In today's Gospel the Pharisees still do not know Jesus, even though he has told them who he is "from the beginning." They remain dead in their sins, because they "belong to this world," because they have reduced both the words and works of Jesus to human categories. Only when they "lift up the Son of Man" on the cross will they realize the truth about him.

God's kindness is always demonstrated in tangible ways. He fed the children of Israel with manna and with quail, but they grew tired of his charity. On the Red Sea road they "complained against God and Moses." They turned their gaze from what is above and preferred death as slaves in Egypt. Their complaints were sins against God. The seraph serpents that bit the people are vivid reminders of the original sin, when Adam and Eve chose being of the world over being from above.

Giving the alms of mercy is always pleasing to God. Long before the cross, the Father had been showing mercy through the signs and wonders he worked for the children of Israel. Just as "many came to believe" Jesus after hearing his discourse with the Pharisees, many of the people on the Red Sea road realized they had sinned against God and Moses. They turned their hearts to what is from above, knowing that only God could save them. Moses mounted a bronze serpent on a pole and placed it before the people for their healing. They had to physically lift their eyes to that which was above them if they wanted to be saved.

If we want to be pleasing to God, we have only to give what we ourselves have received. If we have looked upon Jesus and lived, then we must give life in return. The practice of giving alms keeps our hearts beating with the same rhythm as that of the Sacred Heart. It keeps us on the road that leads to everlasting life.

The economy of salvation has love as its capital, a love that can never be exhausted. Forgiveness of sins depends upon our willingness to accept the currency of God. We must shift our gaze to that which is above. What Jesus and the Father share on that precious height "dispels all evil, washes guilt away, restores lost innocence, brings mourners joy; it casts out hatred, brings us peace and humbles earthly pride."[1]

The earthly household should be managed as the heavenly household is. Just as Jesus and the Father are one, so must we be one with Christ. When Jesus talks about the importance of giving alms, he isn't talking about surplus change but rather about giving that is truly sacrificial. What we have freely received we must freely share.

Precisely because my heart is capable of suffering I want it to give Jesus everything possible.

Wednesday, Week Five
First Reading: Daniel 3:14–20, 91–92, 95
Gospel: John 8:31–42

Yielding to God

In today's reading from the book of Daniel, King Nebuchadnezzar expects Shadrach, Meshach, and Abednego to pay tribute to him by honoring his god. The young men, unafraid and unimpressed, will not serve the king's god; they refuse to bow down and worship the golden statue the king puts before them. They are cast into a man-made hell, where they "[yield] their bodies" as an offering to God. King Nebuchadnezzar actually believes that there is no god who can save them from his power.

Like the three young men, we should content ourselves with doing whatever we have heard from the Father, because there truly is no god in all the land like the God of Shadrach, Meshach, and Abednego. All those who keep to the Lord and walk in his ways need never fear the various hells produced by the wickedness of man.

Jesus' words in the Gospel pay tribute to the young men who were cast into the white-hot furnace. Being a son of Abraham entails doing the "works of Abraham," and these young men trusted God in the same way Abraham did. The Jews listening to Jesus would be true sons of Abraham if they put their trust in Christ.

Jesus shares with them only what he has heard from his Father. The truth to which he testifies does not contradict what Abraham believed; it expands it. The hereditary claim the Jews cling to is insubstantial when compared with the sonship Jesus has in mind.

"If [they] remain in [his] word," they will be not only true children of Abraham but true children of God.

Unfortunately the Jews do not see their need for the freedom that Jesus offers them. They are proud to have never been enslaved. Although John describes them as believers, they are reluctant to pay the price of discipleship. Jesus is not asking them to bow down before him or even to offer a sacrifice. He is simply asking them to take the next step forward toward the day that Moses, the prophets, and even Abraham longed to see.

Like the "Jews who believed in [Jesus]," there are many Christians whose belief fails to translate into action. They have a hereditary claim to God's family based on baptism, but the claim is empty. If they were God's children, they would do the works that Jesus does. For everything the Christian does—socially, politically, financially, sexually—should express trust in the Father.

In today's Gospel Jesus comes begging alms in a way. He is not asking for silver or gold or precious stones or metals. He asks for the hearts of those who believe in him; he asks for their trust. Discipleship is not expensive. We just have to love him.

God granted me, last year, the consolation of observing the fast during Lent in all its rigor.

Thursday, Week Five
First Reading: Genesis 17:3–9
Gospel: John 8:51–59

Prostrate With God

Prayer, fasting, and almsgiving are straightforward ways to "prostrate" ourselves before God. These simple acts are aimed at facilitating the kind of spiritual posture that allows God to speak to us. When we are prostrate before God, we open our lives to his providential care.

This was the effect of Abram's prostration. His willingness to push everything aside for God changed his life forever, even his name. God intended to make Abraham "the father of a host of nations" but wouldn't act without his consent. Bowing low before the Lord was not a punishment but an expression of Abraham's willingness to enter into a covenant by which he and God would be forever bound to one another.

The words from the book of Genesis do not depict Abraham as subservient: God, too, is willing to serve Abraham and his descendants "throughout the ages." Abraham may be prostrate before God, but God is also prostrate before Abraham. This mutual reverence is the binding force of the covenant. Through shared giving and receiving, Abraham and his descendants could look forward to full and abundant life.

Jesus tells the Jews who are with him that keeping his word will prevent them from seeing death. Jesus' words secure the reciprocal nature of the covenant: He speaks not only to us on behalf of the Father but to the Father on behalf of us.

The Jews' response to Jesus' words show that they have forgotten what life with God means. They question him about death because they know that he will die. They have forgotten that real life is found in "every word that comes forth from the mouth of God" (Matthew 4:4, quoting Deuteronomy 8:3). Jesus tries to help them recall God's words so that they can partake of his glory. He points out how divinity can be manifest through flesh and blood. The glory revealed by the paschal mystery is the glory of human life in covenant with God.

Jesus has come to open us up to God's providential care, to a destiny that is more than a geographical location. He has come to establish a lasting pact for us with the Father, a pact that can never be weakened or invalidated by human ignorance or sin. Through his passion, death, and resurrection, Jesus is both God lying prostrate before man and man lying prostrate before God.

The Jews listening to Jesus, and each one of us, must lie prostrate with Jesus. We must give, we must spend, we must relinquish, and we must let go. Every saint has known that the things most valued by the world are ultimately worthless. There is one thing of value, one thing alone that is priceless and makes a person rich, and that is love. The giving of self, the spending of oneself, is the glory of our humanity.

For me to love You as You love me, I would have to borrow Your own Love, and then I would be at rest.

Friday, Week Five
First Reading: Jeremiah 20:10–13
Gospel: John 10:31–42

On the Other Side of the Jordan

Many of the Israelites, including Jeremiah's friends, didn't appreciate what he was calling them to do. As the "breakers of death surged" around him (Psalm 18:5), Jeremiah entrusted his cause to the "LORD of hosts." Jeremiah even hoped to see the vengeance God would take on those seeking to do him harm.

Today it can be difficult to see value in the simple commands of the Gospel. The complexities of life and all its challenges can threaten discipleship with Christ. The Jews listening to Jesus in today's Gospel perceive this. Although many of them already believe in Jesus, the more he explains the purpose of his ministry and his relationship with the Father, the harder it is to follow.

The "whisperings of many" aim at denouncing those who continue following God. Writing off true disciples is easier than writing out a check that's drawn on a commitment to love with all one's heart, all one's strength, and all one's soul. Pointing out the "missteps" of God's children doesn't cost nearly as much as helping them to stand and walking alongside them in their journey to God.

Jesus wants those who follow him to be clear about why he came and clear about whom he serves. In our celebration of the paschal mystery, we not only recall this but also witness the vengeance Jeremiah longed to see. God does not pick up rocks to stone the wicked; he picks up flesh and blood from the Virgin of Nazareth and casts his only begotten Son on the earth, not to injure or destroy it but to bring it life. Jesus is the vengeance God takes on the wicked.

The Jews listening to Jesus are rightly outraged that he would "[make himself] God." But what's even more outrageous is the fact that in Jesus God has made himself a man. The great work Jesus comes to perform is his death on the cross. Through it the Father "puts to utter shame, / to lasting, unforgettable confusion," all those who denounce him. Jesus, in his flesh and blood, willingly accepts the punishment the wicked deserve. He thus severs the cords of the netherworld and frees us all from the snares of death.

On the other side of the Jordan are people who hunger for something greater than the arbitrary values of the world. They came to John the Baptist because their hearts were bankrupted by the ways of the world. When Jesus returns to them, he is empty-handed and poor. All that he has to offer them is his flesh and blood. The currency of his love is acceptable to them, because it's all they have to give him in return.

Jesus alone has the funds the brokenhearted seek. It is from these very funds that we are asked to give alms during the season of Lent.

I also felt a desire of loving only God, of finding my joy only in Him.

Saturday, Week Five
   First Reading: Ezekiel 37:21–28
   Gospel: John 11:45–56

"What Are We Going to Do?"
After five weeks of a catechesis on love that is the season of Lent, the question posed in today's Gospel should be the focus of our thoughts. Like the Sanhedrin, we have read about or heard of the many signs Jesus performed. Now, to enter fully into Holy Week, we need to answer for ourselves the question, "What are we going to do?"

Are we going to continue praying in such a way as to open the depths of our hearts to the communion God longs to share? Are we going to continue fasting in order to drive out the demons that prevent our being fully committed to the works Jesus performs? Are we going to continue giving the alms of charity, as we have received them from the One who completely spent himself in love for us?

The chief priests and the Pharisees once again think Jesus is the problem. They answer the question "What are we going to do?" by formulating a plan to kill him. They never stop to consider whether or not the problem lies within them. They are convinced that "it is better…that one man should die…, so that the whole nation may not perish." They plan to finally put Jesus in his place at the Passover in Jerusalem.

What the Jewish leaders have forgotten is that God longs to return his people to their place, "to the land [he] gave to…Jacob, the land where their fathers lived." This prophecy is more than just an expression of going back; it is about moving ahead to something even greater. Ezekiel's description shows that what

God had in mind was beyond what the Israelites experienced when they first entered in and took possession of the land. Ezekiel describes "an everlasting covenant" of peace, characterized by the fruitfulness of the people and the permanence of the sanctuary.

The works that Jesus performs are signs that the Father's promises to his people are about to be fulfilled. Through the passion and death of Jesus, the Father will establish a new Passover. The feast in Jerusalem to which Jesus goes is the sacrifice of his life on Calvary. He will give his flesh and blood as an offering to the Father, so that he can deliver people from all their sins and cleanse them. The physical body of Jesus will be set up as the new and lasting sanctuary, God's dwelling among people forever.

The Jews who come to Mary know Jesus has raised a man from the dead. That alone should bring them to their knees. Instead they bow to their religious authorities, who actually think they can kill the man who has power over life and death.

Jesus is the Lamb for which the Jews have been searching. He has power over life and death, and in Jerusalem he will show them exactly what that means.

He whose kingdom is not of this world showed me that true wisdom consists in "desiring to be unknown and counted as nothing," in placing one's joy in the contempt of self.

HOLY WEEK

Dear Mother, it seems to me now that nothing could prevent me from flying away, for I no longer have any great desires except that of loving to the point of dying of love.

Palm Sunday of the Lord's Passion
  First Reading: Isaiah 50:4–7
  Second Reading: Philippians 2:6–11
  Gospel Cycle A: Matthew 26:14—27:66
  Gospel Cycle B: Mark 14:1—15:47
  Gospel Cycle C: Luke 22:14—23:56

Standing With Christ

The First Reading beautifully describes the purpose of our proclamation of the Lord's passion. Through the words of the prophet Isaiah, we are primed to anticipate the historical events from the perspective of Christ. It is his interior disposition that dictates the proper manner in which we participate in the liturgy. It is only by entering into his life that we will know how to reply to all that is demanded of us during this striking and solemn celebration.

While each Gospel tells us the story from a unique perspective, they all present a rich body of characters whose lives are caught up in the paschal mystery. Each individual provides a unique vantage point from which to view Christ as he fulfills his Father's mission. However, we must remember that each character is but a starting point; any similarity we share with one is but a way to stand with Christ, who has been raised on high.

While it is important that we take our place within the crowd that first waved palm branches as Jesus entered Jerusalem, we mustn't let ourselves become distracted by the men and women whose roles have been preserved. We may feel like Peter or Pilate, Mary or John, but eventually we must open our ears and stand with Christ, who offered no resistance and did not turn away. Even as we yell, "Crucify him, crucify him," we must not cover our faces, because the words we speak are meant to be heard as Christ heard them. Through our willingness to take our place with the crowd, we experience what it is like to be victim and priest, for each of us is the accuser and the redeemed.

The pageantry of the Passion liturgy of Palm Sunday places the figure of Christ in relief so as to help us set our "face[s] likes flint" and not be shamed by what we celebrate. The solemn entrance begins with a proclamation of the Gospel in order to shape our attentiveness to everything recounted in the liturgy.

We should offer no resistance to the historical details but allow them to deepen our own awareness of the self-emptying of which St. Paul speaks. These striking and often disturbing details highlight the degree to which God is not content to be a spectator of the human condition. God wants to save us by becoming just as we are. As we wave our palms and process into the church, our thoughts should naturally turn to the unimaginable claim of the Passion narrative that Jesus, God's only begotten Son, accepted "death on a cross." The liturgical celebration of this historical truth should not cause us to recoil but to come forward, to approach the place where he stands and receive "a well-trained tongue."

Since it was necessary that the Christ suffer and that He enter through it into His glory, if you desire to have a place by His side, then drink the chalice He has drunk!

Monday of Holy Week
First Reading: Isaiah 42:1–7
Gospel: John 12:1–11

God's Generosity

Jesus returns to the home of Lazarus and dines with him, Martha, and Mary. As the time of his death draws near, Jesus' concern for others has not wavered.

The reverence Mary pays Jesus by anointing him points out how much she has learned by sitting at his feet. There she understands the words of the prophet Isaiah in a whole new way. Jesus has opened her eyes to the light of the God "who created the heavens and stretched them out, / who spreads out the earth with its crops, / Who gives breath to its people / and spirit to those who walk on it." He has opened to her an entirely new way of seeing God, herself, and all of reality.

Although the house is filled with the fragrance of Mary's kindness, Judas smells only lost opportunity. He isn't concerned about Jesus' safety, nor is he concerned for the poor. Judas is concerned with his own profits, and Mary's largesse just eats into them. The outburst Judas makes is not only a gross offense against hospitality; it is also an offense against the generosity of God, who is about to lavish his affection on us through the death of his Son. Where Mary has come into the light, Judas remains in the dungeon of his avarice.

When Jesus intervenes he reveals himself as the chosen one with whom the Lord is well pleased. "He establishes justice on the earth," because his words point out the impoverished condition of humanity. The currency of the economy of salvation is stamped with the image of the cross.

Holy Week begins with a lesson about spending, and the events of this week focus on the Father's revenue and its expenditure. We can learn from Mary about that which is of lasting value, or we can wither in the stinginess of Judas.

Being immersed in the divine economy means standing outside the limited and paltry ways in which men assign value to things that wither and fade and die. Those who refuse to manage their lives according to the economy of love revealed in Jesus' death will be forever poor. They will be with us always, and so, too, our responsibility to them.

Jesus does not ask great actions from us but simply surrender and gratitude.

Tuesday of Holy Week
First Reading: Isaiah 49:1–6
Gospel: John 13:21–33, 36–38

At Table With Jesus

Reclining at table with Jesus can be deeply troubling for us. The words he spoke to his disciples linger: "One of you will betray me." Although we come with the passion of Peter and a willingness to lay down our lives, there remains a voice within that taunts us, "Still, at times, you betray him."

Through this interior voice Satan attempts to enter us. He tries to instill doubts about our ability to glorify the Son of Man through our own redeemed humanity. This voice can only be quieted by recalling the words of the prophet Isaiah: "from [our] mother's womb" God has called each one of us to himself. He has always been our reward and the cause of our strength. The ever deepening experience of the love that formed us into his servants frees us from every nagging doubt and crippling suspicion about our worthiness to receive him.

As we accept the Bread Jesus offers us each Sunday, our gratitude and humility should be rooted in the truth of what he offers. In him our inmost desires are satisfied: As the Responsorial Psalm points out, he is our rock, our stronghold, and our hope (see Psalm 71:3–5). The one who calls us knows truly who we are. He has rescued and saved us. In him we can "never be put to shame." Thus we can return to our places and, like the beloved disciple, lean back to recline with him.

In today's Gospel Jesus sets before us that which is of lasting value. In the simple act of Communion, he continues to extend the substance of his life, in order that "salvation may reach to the ends of the earth." We can take this and rush out into the night, ill-mannered and impolite, with no regard for the gift we have received. Or we can remain with him, perhaps overwhelmed and a bit perplexed but comfortable in his presence. We can "do quickly" the things we must do, or we can hang back for a while, singing of his salvation and proclaiming his wonders.

Judas couldn't distinguish any worth in Jesus' words or in his gesture with the broken bread and shared cup. Judas felt as if he "had toiled in vain, / and for nothing, uselessly, spent his strength." Frustration and resentment prevented him from appreciating what was taking place and blinded him to the glory that was to be revealed before his very eyes. Judas may have held the common purse, but in his heart he was a pauper.

However, the goods which come directly from God, inspirations of the mind and heart, profound thoughts, all this forms a richness to which we are attached as to a proper good which no one has a right to touch.

Wednesday of Holy Week
First Reading: Isaiah 50:4–9a
Gospel: Matthew 26:14–25

"What Are You Willing to Give Me?"

Each day we should awake knowing that "the Lord GOD is my help." We should burn with zeal, "praise the name of God in song," and "glorify him with thanksgiving." In baptism God opened our ears, and he wants to give us "a well-trained tongue," so we can "speak to the weary," those for whom life has become an overwhelming burden. The Holy Spirit provides us with speech, so that we can say the good things people need to hear (see Ephesians 4:29).

This is not how Judas begins the day recounted for us in the Gospel. St. Matthew presents him as a man whose actions are calculated and deliberate. Judas isn't pressured or threatened; of his own volition he goes to the chief priests to learn the price they will pay for the life of the Master. The question Judas asks is gruesome in its frank disregard for the value of human life.

For two days now the Church has asked us to reflect on the person of Judas. He is not an insignificant member of the twelve. He has spent three years following the Lord, witnessing his miracles, and listening to his teachings. Because he has been with Christ throughout his public ministry, the act of betrayal continues to perplex us. Why is he willing to hand Jesus over? When did he lose his way?

Judas's willingness to hand Jesus over is perhaps the gravest example of sin, because Judas wants absolutely nothing to do with what God offers. His rejection of God's love is starker than the original rejection of Adam and Eve. It is not born of ignorance, indifference, doubt, or curiosity; it is a sin against the Holy Spirit, a willful rejection of Love. There is no way back once the ghastly words have been spoken. It truly "would be better for that man if he had never been born."

And yet haven't we all asked, "What are you willing to give me?" We ask this question when we value someone or something more than we value Christ.

The betrayal by Judas is a prelude to the Triduum; the liturgies of the next three days show God's response. Jesus "set [his] face like flint" the moment he stripped himself of glory and was conceived in the Virgin's womb. No one takes his life from him, not even Judas. Jesus freely spends the Father's love by choosing to lay down his life. Betrayal isn't the end of the story; man's salvation is.

May I never lose the second robe of my baptism! Take me before I can commit the slightest voluntary fault.

Holy Thursday, Evening Mass of the Lord's Supper
  First Reading: Exodus 12:1–8, 11–14
  Second Reading: 1 Corinthians 11:23–26
  Gospel: John 13:1–15

"Do You Realize What I Have Done for You?"

"Before the feast of Passover," Jesus knew that the men whom he had called to follow him were not yet ready to experience what he longed to share with them. He knew that the ones who would stand in his place sacramentally needed to be washed in his own blood, in order that no destructive blow should ever come to them.

"On the night he was handed over," Jesus ripped away the veil of the sanctuary. By removing his outer garments, he prepared the apostles for the horror and indignity yet to come. He made it clear that their lives would have meaning and bear fruit only as extensions of his own. "Before the feast of Passover," Jesus manifested his glory by humbling himself before those who would serve him. When he washed their feet, he made divine mercy accessible and reconciliation with God a real possibility.

In the naked vulgarity of his humanity, each priest exists within the mysteries the Church celebrates this night. In every age and for all times, the priest will be the towel Christ uses to wipe away the water that cleanses those having the humility to say, "Lord, I am not worthy to receive you." Each priest was born "before the feast of Passover" and has been given a model to follow. It is the model of a love that takes within itself all human capacity for loving and orders it toward a love that bears itself "to the end."

"Before the feast of Passover," Jesus instituted the Church as a mystery of divine condescension. He changed the most sacred rite of his people into the most sacred rite of all peoples. What was once to be celebrated in "the first month of the year" is now celebrated at every hour throughout the world.

"On the night he was handed over," Jesus gave us a new covenant in his blood. The bread and wine received that night remain a mystery to be celebrated until he comes again. Jesus left as a memorial of his suffering and death the mystery that constitutes the Church and makes it his body.

"Before the feast of Passover," Jesus knew that "his hour had come to pass from this world to the Father" and show the world the perfection of love. "On the night he was handed over," Jesus knew "that the Father had put everything into his power," so he gave it all to his followers.

At the end of the meal Jesus asked a question each one of us must answer: "Do you realize what I have done for you?" The vitality of the Church depends upon the way in which we answer. Jesus has "given [us] a model to follow." This is our obligation and our responsibility; it must be our way of life.

"Before the feast of Passover," Jesus washed the apostles' feet. His hope is that we will do the same for others.

But at the Last Supper, when He knew the hearts of his disciples were burning with a more ardent love for Him who had just given Himself to them in the unspeakable mystery of the Eucharist, this sweet Savior wished to give them a new commandment.

Good Friday
First Reading: Isaiah 52:13—53:12
Second Reading: Hebrews 4:14–16; 5:7–9
Gospel: John 18:1—19:42

"It Is Finished!"

Today's liturgy has us step into Christianity's defining moment. We repeat the story of that incomprehensible horror called the Crucifixion. We contemplate that moment when the Father's servant was "raised high and greatly exalted," on a hill outside Jerusalem. We gather to consider just what it means that Jesus was "cut off from the land of the living" and "smitten for the sin of his people." Today the Church demands the most from us who have spent these past forty days trying to learn what it means to pray, fast, and give alms.

The Second Reading prepares us for the Passion narrative, recalling how Jesus "surrendered himself to death" and "was counted among the wicked." The great high priest, "from whom we have mercy" and "in whom we find grace when we are in need," "always lives to make intercession for" sinners (Hebrews 7:25). Jesus is able to feel our weakness and understand our temptations. In putting his life in our hands, he has put our lives in the hands of his Father.

The disposition of heart needed to rightly venerate Jesus' cross demands that we contemplate this. We must go beyond his being crushed, pierced, and brought low and look upon the fact that this is why he "came into the world."

Perhaps the greatest moment of this day's liturgy is the silence with which it ends, a silence meant to mirror that which occurred when Jesus "handed over the spirit." In the silence of that first Good Friday, the prince of this world was cast out. There was nothing more Satan could say. The lifeless body of the Word hanging on the cross and then held in the arms of his Mother said it all.

"It is finished, Satan! Sin is finished! Your ability to confuse the hearts and minds of the human family about their worth, their dignity, and their place within the heart of God is finished! Yours are not the final words about the essence of what it means to be human."

The moment demands that we willingly remain in the silence. There we uniquely enter into the rest that God took on the seventh day. We are reborn as sons and daughters of the Father. We no longer need a voice coming from the clouds, for in the silence of Good Friday, we know that we are one with him.

Oh Jesus, unspeakable sweetness, change all the consolations of this earth into bitterness for me.

Holy Saturday, the Easter Vigil
  First Reading: Genesis 1:1—2:2
  Second Reading: Genesis 22:1–18
  Third Reading: Exodus 14:15—15:1
  Fourth Reading: Isaiah 54:5–14
  Fifth Reading: Isaiah 55:1–11
  Sixth Reading: Baruch 3:9–15, 32—4:4
  Seventh Reading: Ezekiel 36:16–17a, 18–28
  Epistle: Romans 6:3–11
  Gospel, Cycle A: Matthew 28:1–10
  Gospel, Cycle B: Mark 16:1–8
  Gospel, Cycle C: Luke 24:1–12

What Led Him to This Moment?

The Easter Vigil is the Church's greatest liturgy. Through word, song, and sacred rites, the Church boldly and beautifully sets before her faithful people everything that led Jesus to the moment of the cross and the glory of his resurrection. Beginning with the First Reading and continuing on to the Gospel, we hear much of what has already been recounted throughout the forty days of Lent. The selections from Sacred Scripture not only summarize the instruction in divine love that began on Ash Wednesday but also challenge us to embrace fully just what it means that the stone was rolled away.

Taking our cue then from the sacred text, we can say that what led Jesus to this moment were creation and a rainbow in the sky with a promise not to destroy. It was the election of an aged man and his willingness to sacrifice his son. Jesus comes to a moment built upon an exiled orphan, a burning bush, two stone tablets, manna from heaven, signs and wonders, the Promised Land, and a shepherd boy with the heart of a king.

Jesus was led to this moment by the greeting of an angel, the heroism of a faith-filled Virgin, and the bond between her and the child growing within her womb. It was the joyful greeting of two cousins and the community being formed by them and their children that explain this moment, just as it was the openness to reality on the part of shepherds and the wisdom possessed by men from distant lands. The moment that we celebrate tonight was built upon suffering, sacrifice, and pain, on holy innocents, a flight to Egypt, the school of Nazareth, and thirty years of obscurity.

We come to this moment because of the waters of the Jordan, forty days in the desert, the meeting with John, the attractiveness of a man who talked to God, and the courage of those who followed. We come to this moment because of the twelve apostles, the women who served, the seventy-two, a paralytic man, a demoniac, an ailing child, a demanding mother, a trusting Roman, a hemorrhaging woman, a dead friend, a hungry multitude, a dead boy, a heart moved with pity, a solitary well, a crowded marketplace, an adulterous woman, a rapt synagogue, an angry mob, Adam and Eve, fractured humanity, a conquered people, a complacent governor, and a corrupt king.

Tonight we come to celebrate how all of this and each one of us are responsible for the moment the Church calls the paschal mystery. In the light of this moment, let our minds be ever more one with the mind of the Father and our yes be one with that of his Son.

The Almighty has given them as fulcrum: HIMSELF ALONE; as lever: PRAYER which burns with a fire of love. And it is in this way that they have lifted the world; it is in this way that the saints still militant lift it, and that, until the end of time, the saints to come will lift it.

Notes

The unnumbered entries refer to the quotes at the beginnings and ends of sections.

Introduction

1. John Clarke, trans., *The Story of a Soul: The Autobiography of St. Thérèse of Lisieux*, 3rd ed. (Washington, D.C.: ICS, 1996), p. 174.
2. *Story of a Soul*, p. 156.
3. *Story of a Soul*, p. 105.
4. *Story of a Soul*, p. 277.
5. *Story of a Soul,* p. 190.
6. *Story of a Soul,* pp. 193–194.
7. Preface for Lent I, *Roman Missal*.
8. *Story of a Soul*, p. 99.
9. Preface for Lent III, *Roman Missal*.
10. *Story of a Soul*, p. 208.

Beginning Lent: *Story of a Soul*, p. 189.
Ash Wednesday: John Clarke, trans., *Thérèse of Lisieux: General Correspondence* (Washington, D.C.: ICS, 1988), vol. 2, p. 899.
Thursday After Ash Wednesday: *Story of a Soul,* p. 237.
Friday After Ash Wednesday: *Story of a Soul*, p. 159.
Saturday After Ash Wednesday: *Story of a Soul,* p. 237.

Week One: *Story of a Soul*, p. 242.
Sunday, Cycle A: *Story of a Soul*, p. 166.
Sunday, Cycle B: *Story of a Soul*, p. 240.
Sunday, Cycle C: *Story of a Soul*, p. 149.
Monday: *Story of a Soul*, p. 242.
Tuesday: *Story of a Soul*, p. 243.
Wednesday: *Story of a Soul*, p. 167.
Thursday: *Story of a Soul*, p. 257.
Friday: *Story of a Soul*, p. 220.
Saturday: *Story of a Soul*, p. 227.

Week Two: *Story of a Soul*, p. 218.
Sunday, Cycle A: *Story of a Soul*, p. 207.
Sunday, Cycle B: *Story of a Soul*, p. 112.
Sunday, Cycle C: *Story of a Soul*, p. 250.
Monday: *Story of a Soul*, p. 229.
Tuesday: *Story of a Soul*, p. 105.
Wednesday: *Story of a Soul*, p. 196.
Thursday: *Story of a Soul*, p. 245.
Friday: *Story of a Soul*, p. 126.
Saturday: *Story of a Soul*, p. 256.

Week Three: *Story of a Soul*, pp. 143–144.
Sunday, Cycle A: *Story of a Soul*, p. 99.
Sunday, Cycle B: *Story of a Soul*, p. 112.
Sunday, Cycle C: *Story of a Soul*, p. 187.
Monday: *Story of a Soul*, p. 195.
Tuesday: *Story of a Soul,* p. 267.
Wednesday: *Story of a Soul*, p. 239.
Thursday: *Story of a Soul*, p. 242.
Friday: *Story of a Soul*, pp. 172–173.
Saturday: *Story of a Soul*, p. 223.

Week Four: *Thérèse of Lisieux: Her Last Conversations*, trans. John Clarke
    (Washington, D.C.: ICS, 1977), p. 142.
Sunday, Cycle A: *Story of a Soul*, p. 151.
Sunday, Cycle B: *Story of a Soul*, p. 191.
Sunday, Cycle C: *Story of a Soul*, p. 266.
Monday: *Story of a Soul*, p. 207.
Tuesday: *Story of a Soul*, p. 66.
Wednesday: *Story of a Soul*, p. 172.
Thursday: *Story of a Soul,* p. 199.
Friday: *Story of a Soul*, p. 265.
Saturday: *Story of a Soul*, p. 209.

Week Five: *Story of a Soul*, p. 137.
Sunday, Cycle A: *Story of a Soul*, p. 142.
Sunday, Cycle B: *Story of a Soul*, p. 174.
Sunday, Cycle C: *General Correspondence*, vol. 2, p. 816.
Monday: *Story of a Soul*, p. 83.
Tuesday: *Story of a Soul*, p. 217.
1. *Exultet* (Easter Proclamation).
Wednesday: *Story of a Soul*, p. 210.
Thursday: *Story of a Soul*, p. 256.
Friday: *Story of a Soul*, p. 79.
Saturday: *Story of a Soul*, p. 152.

Holy Week: *Story of a Soul*, p. 214.
Palm Sunday: *Story of a Soul*, p. 133.
Monday: *Story of a Soul*, p. 188.
Tuesday: *Story of a Soul*, p. 233.
Wednesday: *Story of a Soul*, p. 275.
Holy Thursday: *Story of a Soul*, p. 219.
Good Friday: *Story of a Soul*, p. 79.
Holy Saturday: *Story of a Soul*, p. 258.